# HOW TO BE A CAT'S BEST PET

The cat—an animal deeply loved, hated, despised, revered, even worshipped through the ages, today purrs its way into more homes than the dog. The cat will sell you a bill of goods to provide her with delicious food, a warm bed and loads of love and petting—all for mere companionship and a home which she loves more than the people in it.

To understand cats is a mark of keen intelligence, for they do not demonstrate and put on acts except to use man for the cat's good.

Read this book and enjoy your cat more.

> —from the Foreword by Dr. W. A. Young
> Former President, American Cat Association

# THE COMMON SENSE BOOK OF KITTEN AND CAT CARE

*Harry Miller*

**AUTHOR OF**

## The Common Sense Book of Puppy and Dog Care

BANTAM BOOKS

TORONTO · NEW YORK · LONDON · SYDNEY · AUCKLAND

THE COMMON SENSE BOOK OF KITTEN AND CAT CARE

*PRINTING HISTORY*
*Bantam Reference Library edition / November 1966*
*Bantam edition / July 1973*
*Bantam revised edition / September 1987*

ISBN 0-553-26805-8

*Published simultaneously in the United States and Canada*

*Bantam Books are published by Bantam Books, Inc. Its trade-*
*mark, consisting of the words "Bantam Books" and the por-*
*trayal of a rooster, is Registered in U.S. Patent and Trademark*
*Office and in other countries. Marca Registrada. Bantam*
*Books, Inc., 666 Fifth Avenue, New York, New York 10103.*

PRINTED IN THE UNITED STATES OF AMERICA

O     0 9 8 7 6 5 4 3 2 1

# Foreword

by
DR. W. A. YOUNG
Former President of the American Cat Association

The cat—an animal deeply loved, hated, despised, revered, even worshipped by man in lands around the world and thru the ages.

Harry Miller's book, *The Common Sense Book of Kitten and Cat Care*, will provide guidance, ammunition, and source material to any and all who desire to "take a look" at this animal that has survived thru the ages and today purrs his way into homes and hearts of more human beings than the dog, so often referred to as man's best friend.

Why this great spread of sentiment for or against an animal as "gentle as a kitten"?

Cats are among the smartest, if not the most intelligent, animals on the earth. They are not commanded. Feline action is based primarily upon a reason for the cat to do it and not because someone orders the animal to perform.

The fur of a cat may become soiled, but his body is clean and he will bathe and groom himself to a degree of fastidiousness above and beyond that of most humans and do so without taking a course in personal hygiene or playing politics. Yet the cat will sell you a bill of goods provide him with delicious food, a warm bed, and loa of love and petting—all for mere companionship and home that he loves more than the people in it. Yes, he wi move whenever he decides the home across the way more to his satisfaction and will ignore invitations t come home—unless there are sound reasons for him t do so.

To understand cats is a mark of keen intelligence, fo they do not demonstrate and put on acts except to use man for the cat's good.

Read this book and enjoy your cat more.

# Contents

Diarrhea · Constipation · Burns and Scalds
· Cough · Poisoning · First Aid for Swal-
lowed Poisons · Encounters with Skunks ·
Porcupine Quills · Insect Stings · Seizures or
"Fits" · Choking or Swallowing Foreign Ob-
jects · Heatstroke · Wounds and Bleeding ·
Animal Bites

The Cat's Medicine Chest · Quarantine ·
Keeping the Patient Clean · Feeding in Illness · Phoning the Veterinarian · Restraint
· Taking a Cat's Temperature · Administering Medicines

When Do Cats Reach Sexual Maturity? · The
Age to Breed · The Queen in Heat · False
Pregnancy · Arranging the Breeding · Tak-
ing the Queen to the Stud · Courtship and
Breeding · Care during Pregnancy · Prepar-
ing for Delivery · The First Signs of Labor ·
The Delivery · Danger Signs during Delivery
· Postnatal Care · Danger Signs after Deliv-
ery · Caring for the Kittens · Feeding · In-
troducing the Litter Box · The Temporary
Teeth · Preventing Pregnancy: Spaying and
Neutering

The Carrier · Introducing Your Cat to His
Carrier · Preparing for a Journey · Travel by
Car · Staying in Hotels and Motels · Leav-
ing Cats in Parked Cars · Traveling by Bus,

# Introduction

Perhaps you have been thinking lately about acquiring a kitten but you hesitate to undertake the care of an animal you know so little about. You have at the moment no definite idea about the kind you want and, too, the one that may be best suited to your kind of home.

This book tells you how to choose the cat that will be right for your lifestyle—how to feed him and groom him and all about his health care. The book is not a substitute for a veterinarian, but it will increase your awareness and understanding of the charming companion you have chosen to live with.

During the thousands of years in which the cat has lived among human beings, it has been venerated as a deity at certain times and cursed as a demon at others. In ancient Egypt cats were worshipped as sacred creatures. In fact, they were so revered that to kill one deliberately was a crime punishable by death. Herodotus wrote that when a cat died, all the family members shaved off their eyebrows as a gesture of mourning. Cat cemeteries were established along the banks of the Nile where the mummified cats were laid to rest, together with mummified mice to provide food in the afterlife.

Over the centuries, the domestic cat spread from Egypt to Europe. Cats became guardians of the harvest;

and when man ventured out to sea, the cat went with him to keep his ships free of vermin. The good fortunes of cats came to an abrupt end in the Middle Ages when they were thought to be the agents of witchcraft. They were tortured and massacred in every European country for several centuries. By the eighteenth century, though, they were back in favor in most parts of the world. The discoveries of Louis Pasteur in the nineteenth century helped to bolster the cat's position in a suddenly hygiene-conscious Europe. People thought that most animals were dirty and carried disease. The cat—the paragon of meticulous grooming—became the exception.

Today, according to a recent study sponsored by the Pet Food Institute, cats now outnumber dogs for the first time. More than fifty million of these charming and mysterious creatures reside in twenty-four million American households. Cats make perfect pets for many reasons: they are gentle and affectionate, they are intelligent, they are not demanding, they are immaculate and fastidious, they are exotic-looking, they are easily trained to a litter box and don't have to be walked. Cats are extremely adaptable—they can live long and happy lives in small apartments or on large estates.

# 1
# The History of the Cat

Cats belong to the class known as *Mammalia*, or mammals. They can be traced back to a primitive ancestor, *Miacis*, a small, tree-living creature of the late Eocene period some forty-five to fifty million years ago. Resembling the civet, *Miacis* had a long, fur-covered body, short legs, and a long, heavy tail. Its paws had catlike retractile claws that made tree climbing very easy.

From about forty million years ago, the Miacids evolved into the ancestors of the various carnivores known today, among them the *Canidae*, or dog family, which includes wolves, jackals, coyotes, foxes, and dogs; and the *Felidae*, or cat family, which includes lions, tigers, leopards, jaguars, lynx, ocelots, and domestic cats.

The *Felidae* came in a wide range of sizes and coloration—big cats and little cats; some self-colored, others spotted or striped for concealment in the wild. As the centuries rolled on, they were divided into the large cats, of the genus *Panthera*, and the small cats (like the domestic cat), of the genus *Felis*. Thus, while cat and dog are not exactly kissing cousins, at least they can boast a common ancestor.

The early history of the domestic cat may forever remain a mystery impossible to resolve because of conflicting theories and opinions. This, however, is quite a usual state of affairs when one attempts to trace any animal from prehistoric times. We cannot know definitely what happened so long ago; consequently, we must resort to inference.

Ancient Egypt, China, and India all played an important part in the cat's long journey into the present. As far as we know, cats were first domesticated in Egypt, most likely around 3000 B.C. The first species to be domesticated probably was the African wild cat *(Felis libyca)*, an animal that roamed over most of North Africa and Asia at the time. *F. libyca* was an agile, sandy-colored cat with pale markings similar to today's domestic tabbies. Another larger jungle cat, *Felis chaus*, also may have been involved in the origin of the domestic cat.

The tombs of the pharaohs have supplied a certain amount of definite information, especially the discovery there of mummified cats laid away with such care as to suggest that they were highly regarded by the Egyptian people. The Egyptians also left carved figurines of cats, which they considered gods to be worshipped. They called the little cat "Mu" or "Mau" and punished with death anybody who dared kill one. Worship and work went hand in hand in those early times—the cat might be a god, but he was expected to work for his keep. So the Egyptians trained him to destroy the rats and mice that infested their granaries, and later to retrieve waterfowl shot with bow and arrow.

Cats were domesticated in India and the Far East in ancient times, but at a later date than in Egypt. They were known in China before 2000 B.C., although some authorities believe they were not considered domestic animals until A.D. 400. The Chinese admired cats for their rat-catching abilities, but they also believed that cats brought poverty into a household. This calamity could be prevented, however, by paying homage to little pottery statues of cats squatting and gazing into the distance. In India, legends and fables about cats are found in some of the great Hindu epics, among them the *Mahabharata*, the *Ramayana*, and the *Panchatantra*. Their cunning qualities were recounted, and they were praised for being "mouse eaters."

Eventually domestic cats were taken out of Egypt to Europe in spite of a law forbidding their exportation. Cats were stolen, most likely by Roman soldiers and Phoenician traders, and taken throughout the Mediterranean area. Egyptian soldiers were urged to pick up any cats they found in foreign lands and bring them back home to Egypt.

It is easy to see how wars in both ancient and modern times played an important role in the distribution of animals to different countries. When Caesar invaded Britain in 55 B.C., he was impressed by the local mastiff dogs that fought beside their masters, and he sent several to Rome to fight lions, tigers, and bears in the amphitheaters. Another example is the sacred Pekingese, which escaped from China in the nineteenth century when invading English soldiers looted the Imperial Palace at Peking during the Boxer Rebellion and took a few good dogs back to England.

The cat's stature was greatly increased at the end of the eleventh century during the military expeditions known as the Crusades. The ships of Crusaders returning from the Holy Land swarmed with hordes of plague-bearing rats, and cats were recognized as the best of all possible deterrents. Monks in the monasteries valued them as guardians of their storehouses. Captains of sailing vessels thought cats were endowed with extraordinary powers that would protect them on the seas; they took them along to guard their stored food from rats as well.

The cat's fortunes changed abruptly in the late Middle Ages when it became associated with a pagan fertility cult immortalizing the Norse goddess Freya, which was experiencing a revival in the Rhineland. Because cats played a role in the rites of this cult, the Christian church launched a campaign against them. Cats were tortured, burned, and slaughtered throughout Europe in the name of religion. When the church sanctioned the persecution of witches, a great many guiltless people went to the gallows or were burned at the stake, simply because they owned cats and were thought to be witches. Nothing was too horrible for the creature that was worshipped in ancient Egypt, and the torment and butchery continued for the next four hundred years or so.

Cats came to North America with the Pilgrims on the *Mayflower*. Although they were valued by early settlers as killers of vermin, they became associated with witchcraft and superstition, too, in New England. Legend had it that when a cat was allowed near the body of a dead person, it would steal the soul and the corpse would then become a vampire. Many people believed that when a black cat crossed your path, you had to cross your fingers to offset trouble. A great many cat phobias and superstitions still survive in the United States.

Cats had their good and bad times until the eighteenth century when people began to recognize their usefulness again, and they became favorably regarded in most parts of the world. The militant humanitarians began to reiterate the teachings of Saint Francis of Assisi that animals were not gods to be worshipped nor things of evil to be persecuted, that they were sentient beings entitled to man's protection. Many years were to elapse before this precept began to bear fruit. But the animals did gradually benefit from it, and in 1835 the dedicated humanitarians in England put on the official books a law designed to punish those who mistreated animals of any kind.

From that time forth, even as he continued to ply his trade as incomparable hunter of the smaller rodents, the cat gained status as pet and companion. Slowly but surely he charmed his way into the hearts of the people as his qualifications for companionship came to be recognized. His keepers found him clean to the point of fastidiousness, affectionate, graceful, decorative, and quiet about the house; in fact, a gentle stay-at-home—all this, and a willing workman whenever and wherever his services might be needed.

# 2
# The Selection
# of a Cat

No other animal is as charming and graceful as a cat. Whatever your personal circumstances, cats make great pets because they are affectionate, they have fastidious habits, and unlike dogs, they don't have to be walked. Whether you are young or old, single or married, active or infirm, or whether you live in the city, the suburbs, or the country, a cat is easy to care for.

As a pet owner you'll have certain responsibilities to both your cat and your community. The cat is entitled to kindness, proper nutrition, regular grooming, training, and humane treatment. Cats are generally inexpensive to keep, but you will be responsible for routine medical checkups and having the cat immunized against certain infectious diseases. You will also need to provide other things such as a litter box, a scratching post, a bed, toys, feeding dishes, and a sturdy cat carrier.

Cats should be kept indoors; when they do go out, they should be kept under control and not permitted to roam free to disturb other people, to fight with other animals, or to breed indiscriminately.

## DECISIONS TO MAKE

Once you have decided to own a cat, there are a number of choices to be made. Cats come in many different shapes and colors, and there is no reason why you shouldn't get the kind you are most attracted to, since you are making a commitment that could last from fifteen to twenty years.

Do you like a cat with a svelte, fine-boned body and slender legs like a Siamese or Oriental Shorthair, or one with a large and sturdy body set on short, strong legs like a Persian or British Shorthair? Do you like a long, wedge-shaped head with slanting, almond-shaped eyes, or is a big, round head with full cheeks and large round eyes your cup of tea? Do you like hair that is sleek and glossy or long and silky? Do you like unusual colors—lavender smoke, cinnamon, chestnut silver, chinchilla golden—or traditional colors—white, black, blue, red, cream? Do you want a solid-colored cat or an exotic-looking one with spots and stripes? Chapter 16, "The Cat Breeds," will give you information about thirty-five breeds that come in many different color varieties and markings.

Here are some other things to consider before choosing your feline companion.

### SHOULD YOU CHOOSE A PUREBRED OR MIXED-BREED?

What do we mean by a breed? As far as cats are concerned, a breed is a group of cats, more or less uniform in size and structure, produced and maintained by selective breeding. Man selects the cats that have the qualities he admires and, by breeding them over a period of time, gets kittens that look alike and that, when grown and mated, will produce offspring like themselves. That is why this is known as selective breeding—man selects the male and female he thinks, mated together, will produce the type of cat he wants.

A purebred is a cat of only one breed, that is, both its parents are the same kind of cat. The kittens of a purebred Persian male and a purebred Persian female, for instance, are purebred Persians. A mixed-breed is a cat whose ancestors are of mixed-breed origins or unknown.

The fact that mixed-breeds cost very little or frequently are given away, whereas purebreds often cost quite a sum, suggests certain differences. Cost does not always mean value, but it is a guide. There has to be a reason why we can get a mixed-breed for little or nothing, and why we must pay hundreds of dollars for a purebred cat.

Mixed-breeds are often sold for very little or given away because someone wants to get rid of them. Usually bred by accident or neglect, they are an unnamed product with no market value. The purebred, on the other hand, has been bred from selected parents and raised under the best conditions for health and good development. Each purebred has its own standard of perfection, or written description, by which it is judged. The standard is a detailed list of characteristics that together describe the "ideal," a word picture of the perfect Abyssinian, Burmese, Himalayan, Persian, Siamese, and so forth. Therefore, when you buy a purebred, you know more nearly what you are getting. You can reasonably predict the cat's size, type, conformation, coat length, markings, personality, and other general traits.

When you get a mixed-breed, you are getting uncertain quality. Some mixed-breeds do closely resemble certain purebreds, but it's difficult to determine what others

will look like when they mature. Still, the mixed-breed
heart is in the right place, and he will give just as much
devotion and affection to you. Far better a mixed-breed
than no cat at all! Many a happy home has been blessed
with fascinating-looking, steady, and devoted creatures
of dubious ancestry.

The expense of raising any kitten, whatever its lineage or background, will be roughly the same, although
a poorly nourished or unhealthy one may need a lot of
veterinary attention early on, and this is something to
keep in mind.

## WHICH SEX SHOULD YOU CHOOSE?

If you are not interested in breeding and plan to
have your cat spayed or neutered, there is little difference
between a male and female since both make wonderful
pets. Owning an unspayed female can be annoying when
she starts having frequent heat periods after she reaches
six to eight months of age. During these periods, she will
become very restless and start "calling" loudly to attract
the attention of males in the area.

When an unneutered male becomes mature at about
nine months of age, he starts getting possessive about his
territory (your home), and may spray the furniture and
other objects with strong-scented urine. In addition,
many whole tomcats are more likely to roam the neighborhood and become involved in fierce battles with other
males. If you are not planning to breed your cat, having a
female spayed or a male neutered will avoid accidental
matings and unwanted litters, and will result in a more
affectionate housepet.

## SHOULD YOU GET A SHORTHAIR OR LONGHAIR?

All cats need some kind of regular grooming. When choosing your cat, the length of coat is important because you will have to care for it yourself. Grooming the smooth and slinky-looking shorthairs is a fairly easy procedure. Longhairs are more fluffy and tend to leave more hair around the house. They require daily combing and brushing since their coats become matted when they do not receive regular attention.

## SHOULD YOU CHOOSE A KITTEN OR AN ADULT?

Kittens adapt quickly to new homes, children, other pets, and it's charming to watch them grow up. A kitten, however, requires constant supervision. He must be fed several times a day and trained. The well-trained mature cat, on the other hand, can get along with one daily meal if need be, and he has already learned to conduct himself properly in the home.

You know exactly what you are getting when you acquire a grown cat; his disposition is established, as it were, and dispositions do vary among individuals. You may have read that the various cat breeds have different characters—that some are more affectionate, more easily trained than others. Cat breeds do have distinct temperaments; however, it is also true that the disposition of an adult depends to a great extent upon the way it has been brought up.

Since cats are great homebodies, an adult cat may have become so attached to his owners that he finds it hard to adjust to a strange family and unfamiliar surroundings. The young kitten has nothing to forget. He

**11**

adjusts with the greatest of ease to your home and your ways. In short, he is all yours to a degree that the mature cat may never be. But he does need a reasonable amount of care. Feeding and training take time, and possible illness during the growing period may involve a certain amount of risk. Raising a kitten, however, is an interesting and enjoyable adventure that no one need fear. Today, you can find knowledgeable veterinarians practically everywhere to help you not only to cure but to prevent ailments and diseases. To watch a young kitten grow and learn, to develop physically and mentally, is a delightful experience.

## WHICH BREED IS BEST?

Because the various breeds have altogether different temperaments and characteristics, it is important to choose the right cat for your personality and lifestyle.

If you want an agile and energetic cat, consider getting a shorthair; if you fancy a calm, dignified animal, you'd do better with a longhair. A person who stays at home most days might appreciate a sweet and affectionate cat such as the Russian Blue, the Korat, the Bombay, the Singapura, the Cornish Rex, the Manx, or the Persian—all of which become very attached to their owners. Conversely, a working person may want an adaptable breed like the American Shorthair, the British Shorthair, or the American Wirehair, instead of a breed like the Siamese, the Oriental Shorthair, or the Burmese—all of which may resent being left alone.

People with children or people with other pets should also look for an adaptable, gentle, and outgoing cat rather than one that is unfriendly or temperamental. Those who are attracted by "different looking" breeds might consider the Egyptian Mau, the Ocicat, the Oriental Shorthair, the Birman, the Cornish or Devon Rex, the Scottish Fold, the Himalayan, or the Persian—all of which come in exotic colors or coat patterns.

## WHERE SHOULD YOU GET YOUR KITTEN OR CAT?

When you have decided which breed you'd like to own, the next consideration is where to get it. Many kittens are sold through local pet stores. The shop owners usually buy kittens from nearby breeders or occasionally offer a referral service through local breeders. More frequently, however, they buy litters of kittens produced by commercial breeders. It is possible to get a healthy kitten of good quality from pet stores, especially if they offer local breeder referrals. But if the kittens were obtained from an out-of-state commercial breeder, their quality and health may be questionable. The shop owner may have no idea of the temperament, health, or background of the kittens' parents. Thus forewarned, make your selection contingent upon having the kitten examined by your veterinarian.

The best source of pedigreed kittens is the reputable private breeder or cattery. You can contact your local cat club or ask your veterinarian to give you the names of reputable breeders in your area. Pedigreed cats can also be found through advertisements in the local newspapers, in periodicals devoted to cats, at cat shows, or by referrals from friends who own purebred cats. A visit to a cat show lets you see lots of different cats and kittens, and to chat with their owners. Although some of the kittens at the show may be for sale, it's preferable to wait and observe the entire litter at home.

Perhaps a neighbor or friend has unwanted kittens

that he wants to find homes for. And keep in mind that humane shelters and adoption agencies have cats of all ages that can be adopted for a small fee or voluntary contribution. Most of these are mixed-breeds, but occasionally purebreds are available, too.

### HOW CAN YOU TELL IF YOUR KITTEN IS HEALTHY?

When you visit a breeder for the purpose of selecting a kitten, you will find the litter of perhaps four or five comfortably housed in a box or bed in a secluded area.

The physically sound kitten is active, bright, and responsive. Even at an early age he tries to make his way around the box as if to find out what is going on around him. Curiosity, you know, is a sign of intelligence. It is safe to say that all cats are curious and intelligent, but like animals the world over, some are smarter and more inquisitive than others. The kitten that pushes aside his brothers and sisters in the nest in a comically aggressive manner is the one to watch.

The next thing to look for is good health: the kitten with clear, bright, wide-open eyes as opposed to watery, squinting, or sticky eyes; a soft and supple skin and coat, with no fleas or bare patches, and clean all over, especially inside the ears and around the vent. The healthy nose is cool and moist, the tongue pink. Beware of the young one with a runny nose, and be sure he is not deaf.

In selecting a kitten you will want to consider not only his apparent health, but the health of his littermates and parents as well. You should not take the kitten home with you until he is at least six to eight weeks old, when he should be completely weaned from his mother and litter-box trained.

A reputable breeder will not sell a sick kitten. But

should a breeder try to hurry you into taking a kitten even slightly below par "before anyone else gets it," head for the nearest exit!

## WHAT DOCUMENTS SHOULD
## THE BREEDER PROVIDE?

If you decide to buy a purebred kitten, the breeder should give you the following papers:

- The kitten's pedigree or family tree.
- A Certificate of Registration. Pedigreed cats should be registered with a cat fancier's organization under an individual name. The certificate will also list the cat's registration number, his breed and color, and the names of his parents. It is your responsibility to pay the nominal fee to have ownership transferred to your name.
- Proof of temporary or permanent vaccination against several infectious diseases, including feline panleukopenia (FPL) and three upper respiratory disorders—rhinotracheitis, pneumonitis, and infection by calicivirus. It is also advisable to request a blood test for feline leukemia (FeLV). Last year, a new vaccine to protect cats against this virus became available. You should discuss this with your veterinarian.
- A health record, specifying the dates of any wormings.
- A list of foods that the cat is eating.
- A written health guarantee that the kitten may be returned or replaced within a specific time period if it shows signs of illness. As soon as you obtain your cat, you should have it checked by a veterinarian.

# 3

# The Two- to Four-Month-Old Kitten

The period from two to four months is when the majority of kittens are taken from catteries to their new homes. It is a critical period. Because of the little one's growing awareness of what goes on in the world about him, he needs very careful handling.

Before you bring your kitten home, it is wise to have certain supplies and equipment on hand to make his first days more comfortable. Most can be purchased at local pet stores or supermarkets. Things such as a cat bed, litter box, fresh cat litter and a scoop, food and water dishes, a scratching post, and a few toys should be ready and waiting for the new arrival.

## THE BED

As soon as the kitten arrives at his new home, he should find a bed or basket of his own, placed in a quiet

**17**

area, removed from possible drafts and preferably a few inches off the floor. Floors can be drafty. Even though you cannot feel the draft, chances are it is there just the same, and it can be deadly! Under certain conditions animals can stand heat and cold, but they cannot stand drafts.

The bed may be a fancy ready-made kind, a wicker basket, or only a simple cardboard carton with an opening cut into the side. See that it is lined with a washable pillow, a blanket, or something cozy into which the kitten can nestle to relax or sleep as he prefers. Up to this time he has had his mother and littermates to snuggle up to, but they will not be there anymore.

### FOOD AND WATER DISHES

Every cat should have his own feeding dish and water bowl. Pet feeding dishes are made of stainless steel, plastic, ceramic, porcelain, and pottery. Pick a style that is easy to clean and heavy enough not to slide across the floor while the cat eats or tip over easily. The food dish should be rather shallow: cats do not like to eat out of deep bowls. Don't forget to have food on hand for the kitten's first meal.

### LITTER BOX, LITTER, AND SCOOP

A litter box is a very important item to the cat. Innumerable cats of all ages spend their entire lives indoors— that is why they make satisfactory companions for those who occupy apartments. Consequently, you must provide an easily accessible, sanitary toilet indoors.

Various types of litter boxes are available at pet shops. The most common kind is a shallow, rectangular-shaped plastic box that measures twelve by eighteen inches. Other styles have detachable lids or hoods for cats that scratch up a lot of litter or those that like privacy. If you are getting a young kitten, start with the standard rectangular box, making sure that it is shallow enough for the little one to climb over the edges. Whatever the size or type of box used, it must lend itself to efficient cleaning and deodorizing.

Although shredded newspapers and sand can be used in the box, most cat owners prefer commercial clay litter because it is absorbent and easy to dispose of. You will also need a slotted scoop designed to remove fecal matter from the box so you don't have to handle soiled litter. To control odors, sprinkle a little baking soda or litter deodorant on the bottom of the box before pouring in the litter. Wash the box thoroughly with soap and water each time you change the litter.

## SCRATCHING POST

As your kitten begins to get acquainted and run about, he may claw whatever furniture or carpets happen to be within reach. You cannot stop this sometimes annoying action; it is instinctive. So go along with it. Make the best of it by providing a definite place for him to scratch.

The ideal scratching post is sturdy, covered with a rough surface, and tall enough to let a cat stretch to his full height to claw. You can buy a scratching post or make one yourself by covering a solid wooden post with coarse-textured carpeting.

## TOYS

Your kitten's favorite form of fun and exercise up to now has been to frolic and play-fight with his littermates. Now that he has been removed from this setting, he needs a few toys to keep him amused. Most pet stores have a variety of toys to choose from—fur or felt mice, sponge and lattice balls, catnip-filled sacks and soft cloth toys, pompons and furry tails tied to strings, and peacock feathers. Choose secure toys that cannot get caught in the kitten's throat or swallowed whole, toys that do not have metal squeakers, bells, or glued-on parts which he can easily remove. You don't have to spend a lot of money to keep your cat amused. Ping-pong balls, cardboard toilet paper tubes, and old knotted socks make great playthings.

## BRINGING YOUR CAT HOME

Plan to pick up your new kitten when you have plenty of time to spend allaying his fears and to strengthen the bond between you—on a Saturday morning or during vacation if you work, for example. The safest way to bring him home is in a carrier. Don't just wrap him in a blanket and hold him in your arms; he can easily squirm free. Choose a well-ventilated case that has a secure latch. There are many different kinds of carriers available, and if you intend to take your cat on trips in the car or to shows, it is worth investing in a sturdy, lightweight, adult-size carrier.

Buffer the floor with a soft piece of blanket or finely shredded newspapers to absorb moisture in case the baby urinates or vomits his dinner en route. Whether the journey home is long or short, hold the carrier carefully; and if you are traveling by car, try to minimize jolt and sidesway.

As soon as you arrive home, take the kitten out of the carrier and let each family member greet the new arrival. All his essential items should be in their proper places. Show the kitten his litter box. Keep children and other pets away for the moment. Do not expect the newcomer to play just now. He is bewildered, his erstwhile jauntiness gone, his spirit dejected. He misses his mother and littermates. He feels strange and tired. Let him alone. After a good nap, he may decide that this new life is not so bad after all, and he may wake up as hungry as a little bear.

Let him explore his new surroundings at his own pace, but watch to see that he doesn't get into trouble. And see that he can easily find his litter box, food, and water.

### HOW TO FEED

It is customary for the breeder to give you a menu sheet explaining when, what, and how much the kitten has been fed. This is valuable. Follow its directions explicitly and the baby will hardly know he has changed homes. You or your veterinarian may decide to change the diet eventually, but it's wise to wait until the kitten adjusts to his new surroundings. You will find more about nutrition in Chapter 7.

At this age periodic rest is essential, which means that after eating the kitten should be left alone. For the sake of his digestion do not encourage the youngster to play or exert himself unnecessarily. And be sure his litter box is handy, always in the same place so he will know where to find it. Ordinarily, he will use the box directly after eating.

## HANDLING

Handling at this age is considered vital to the development of a kitten's personality because of his rapidly growing awareness. It was once believed that young kittens should be left alone as much as possible and handled only when necessary. Time has taught us that the right sort of handling helps to inspire confidence and in that way equip the kitten to enjoy life more fully as a member of the family. In short, if he is to live with people, he must learn to associate with them at an early age.

The right sort of handling is extremely gentle, deliberate, and quiet rather than abrupt, jerky, or boisterous. In the nest the queen is quick to note excessive attention or rough handling; then she is apt to pick up her babies by the scruff of the neck and carry them one by one to a more secluded place. She knows how to pick them up in this manner without hurting them (the term "queen" refers to an unneutered female cat, especially one used for breeding purposes.)

The general rule, then, is to handle the newcomer often and with great care. Pick him up gently, put him down gently. Stroke him down the back and under the chin so he will learn to recognize your intentions as friendly. He can be injured or frightened if teased or dropped. Make every effort to gain his confidence; it will render future training and management much easier.

### HOW TO PICK UP THE CAT

Because the cat's body is soft and pliable, we frequently pick him up any old way. Look out: he can be hurt or frightened. Use both hands gently. Approach him from the side; place one arm around his forelegs, the other around his hind legs or beneath his abdomen. Hold him in your arms as you would a baby, supported so comfortably that he is not prompted to escape. Or, instead of placing one arm around the forelegs, insert the flat of your hand under his chest between the forelegs. This too gives support to the entire body in such a manner that the cat will not try to squirm free.

When you put him down, lower him gently with all four feet meeting the floor at the same time to avoid strain. Some cats are great lap-sitters. When people tire of holding them, they just let them jump off. The ground shock of landing suddenly on the floor is not in the best interest of kittens whose ligaments are not as strong as they will be later. When releasing the lap-sitter, then, straighten out your legs and let him slide down slowly.

### MAKING YOUR HOME SAFE

A kitten's inquisitive nature can lead to trouble, even in a seemingly safe environment like your home. There are dangers galore indoors that need not be hazards if we think about what could happen and then take steps to prevent it. Prevention in innumerable instances is a very simple procedure.

Hanging cords of any kind are an invitation to play. Whatever happens to be attached to the other end may come crashing down on the poor kitten's head. Old or frayed electric light cords, low-hanging within reach of the playful youngster, may prove dangerous. On rare occasions cats have been shocked by touching exposed sections of electric wires.

Crawling into dark or secluded places is a favorite feline diversion; keep drawers, closet doors, cupboards, oven doors, dishwasher doors, clothes washers and dryers, luggage, and cartons closed. All of these are warm napping places in which your kitten could be imprisoned.

Windowsills are for sunbathing when the windows are closed or when screens are securely fastened, otherwise the kitten could fall out. An apartment terrace or rooftop garden is excellent for airing, but safe only when the cat is on leash. Parapets are a safeguard for people but not for cats. When chasing insects or leaves, cats do not look where they are going. Intent upon catching anything that moves, they leap to the parapet and over they go!

All over the house from attic to basement, little items can lie unobserved on the floor—pins and needles, buttons and paper clips, rubber bands, bits of foil or cellophane, tiny cuttings of screen wire and tacks, many other things we seldom realize are ready and waiting to be picked up and possibly swallowed by a kitten looking for something to play with.

Watch tabletops, shelves, and bedroom bureaus with their array of breakable objects. Ever ready to jump up and investigate, cats are apt to knock off and break small items and then step on the shattered glass. Keep trash cans securely closed and look inside opaque trash bags before sealing them. Make sure that both indoor and garden plants are not poisonous to cats.

Holidays like the Fourth of July can on occasion be uncomfortable for a cat when municipalities stage exhibitions of loudly exploding fireworks. Animals differ in their response to noise: some never turn a hair while others become frightened. When you live close to one of these displays, keep your cat under surveillance lest he find his way into some outlandish hideout where it takes the patience of Job to find him.

Christmas can be hazardous for a cat—there are so many intriguing things within reach. The scintillating gadgets on the tree catch his eye, and he cannot resist the temptation to reach up with his paw and set them swinging. Down they come to break into a thousand pieces that the kitten can pick up on his feet and eventually swallow.

### THE FIRST HEALTH EXAMINATION

It is essential to take your cat for a complete veterinary examination within forty-eight hours after he enters your home. He may need to be vaccinated against panluekopenia, rhinotracheitis, calici virus, pneumonitis, and perhaps rabies and feline leukemia. Depending on your kitten's age, he may have received some or all of the necessary temporary or permanent inoculations. If you obtained a health record from the breeder, show it to the veterinarian so he or she can determine if additional shots are required. Take along a fresh stool sample; the veterinarian will want to examine it microscopically to determine if worms are present.

### SELECTING A VETERINARIAN

If you don't already have a veterinarian, ask the kitten's breeder or your cat-owning neighbors for recommendations. The local veterinary association can also give you the names of veterinarians in your area. You will find conscientious and competent veterinarians conveniently located almost everywhere.

It's wise to choose and get acquainted with the veterinarian before trouble occurs. Today's veterinarians are busy professionals; they do not often go to one's home. Their more complicated equipment for examination and treatment is office-bound, so you must go to them.

Learn if the veterinary hospital is located within a short drive from your home; find out what the office hours are, and whether it is possible to obtain emergency care after hours, or on weekends and holidays. Once inside the hospital, see if the facilities are clean, bright, and pleasant-smelling. Does the veterinarian handle your cat carefully? Is he or she willing to discuss problems, treatments, and fees? Is the staff courteous and cheerful and, most important, kind to animals?

The important point is to seek professional assistance before an ailment is advanced and the treatment unnecessarily difficult or expensive. Don't forget that, like everything else these days, the cost of animal care has increased considerably. Some large cities have pet clinics for those unable to pay normal fees. Your local humane organization can direct you to these.

### EARLY TRAINING

As soon as the kitten enters your home, you should begin litter box and scratching post training.

### INTRODUCING THE LITTER BOX

Housebreaking or, to be more exact, litter box training is a fairly simple procedure based upon the cat's natural desire for cleanliness. It is not so much a problem of training as it is of giving the kitten an opportunity to keep his quarters clean. Most breeders inaugurate this type of training while the kittens are still in the nest.

For the first few weeks, the queen attends to the toilet of her young ones by licking them off at frequent intervals as required. If the breeder places a litter box in or near the nest after the kittens are walking, the queen will show her brood how to dig into the litter box and then cover up the hole to hide their wastes.

If your cat is slow to catch on to what the box is for, lift him gently into it and scratch the litter with your finger, or take his tiny paw in your hand and help the baby to dig. Once the box is used, its odor will prompt the kitten to use it again.

For a limited time, while the youngster is going through the learning process, leave a small amount of soiled litter in the box; this will induce him to visit the same spot again. And needless to say, the box should always be available in the same place, preferably in a rather secluded spot.

When you give your new kitten a certain amount of freedom in the house, you may see him looking round and round as if to locate the proper place. If he chooses the wrong spot, pick him up and scold "Thomas, no!" and place him in his box.

Even though the odor helps to instill the idea of what the box is used for, it should not be allowed to become really dirty. Kittens and cats of all ages do not like to use dirty boxes. Renew the litter frequently and wash the box thoroughly with hot, soapy water. Wash your hands after handling the box; a disease called toxoplasmosis can be transmitted to humans through contact with feces of infected cats. More about toxoplasmosis can be found in Chapter 11, "Practical Home Care."

There will be mistakes at first. Especially when a kitten is in a new home, he may soil rugs or carpets in his path as he runs about. Be very sure to clean and deodorize such spots, otherwise they will be used for the same purpose again and again. Wash the soiled spots thoroughly with soap and water, then rub with a vinegar solution (one ounce of vinegar in one pint of warm water) or a commercial pet odor neutralizer (such as Nilodor) to eliminate any lingering smells.

## SCRATCHING POST TRAINING

A cat scratches both horizontal and vertical objects for several reasons: for exercise, to sharpen his claws and remove frayed or loose pieces of sheaths, and to mark his territory. Scratching is an inherited trait of all cats that can be performed as early as five weeks of age. Scratching motions can be noticed even when kittens are declawed early in life. To prevent your kitten from damaging household furnishings and other valuable objects indoors, you must *immediately* provide him with a scratching post. Once a cat starts to scratch an object or area, he does not change easily.

A scratching post is a sturdy vertical piece of wood, mounted on a pedestal, and covered with coarse-textured carpeting or rough material such as bark, cork, canvas, or burlap. Some are scented with catnip to make them more tempting. In addition to being firm, the post should be at least twelve inches high so your cat can rest his weight on his hind legs and use his forepaws to claw. The post should be kept near his bed since cats are most likely to scratch upon waking.

Ideally, the scratching post should be introduced as soon as the kitten enters your home so he becomes accustomed to using it. Occasionally, a kitten takes to the post without formal introduction while others have to be shown what it is for. As soon as your kitten starts to scratch something that's off-limits, tell him "No!" loudly and firmly, and squirt him with a water pistol or plant mister. Take him to the scratching post, hold his forelegs up, then carefully draw them downward to show him how you want him to behave. Once he gets the idea, he may forget all about carpets, draperies, and upholstered chairs and stick to his own special substitute.

## ONE CAT OR TWO

Suppose you already have one cat and you have decided to get another. Is it safe to bring in a second cat? Yes, especially if both pets will be spayed or neutered.

When attempting to bring a new cat into the household, be sure it is in perfect health. Have the newcomer checked thoroughly by your veterinarian so you don't expose your present cat to parasites, skin infections, or diseases.

The first step is to let the newcomer snoop around the house by himself to get the scent of the pet that already lives there. The old-timer, of course, should be isolated from the new cat. The next step is to confine the newcomer in a cage and let the old-timer see him and get his scent. Confining both cats in adjoining cages is an excellent form of introduction because it permits the two to see each other and lets the owner observe the reaction of one to the other.

Pay generous attention to the old-timer at first to avoid jealousy or fighting. If the new arrival gets all the attention, the old-timer may refuse to eat and may become destructive. Days or weeks may elapse before the two strangers become adjusted to each other and decide to be friends. You cannot hurry this period of adjustment since one or the other, perhaps both, may be nervous and apprehensive. Should the two be introduced too quickly, they may fight, and it will take considerably longer to establish relations.

### CAT AND DOG

Suppose you already own a dog. Is it advisable to bring in a cat as a second pet? Contrary to the time-honored tales of cat and dog enmity, the two often live together in perfect harmony. The dog may never relinquish his favorite sport of chasing cats, but he generally will not exercise in the house what he considers his rightful prerogative against his furry companion. Once well acquainted, cat and dog become fast friends.

The full-grown dog rarely resents a young kitten; it seems to awaken his protective instinct for an animal so tiny and helpless. Not so the mature cat, which the dog may regard as a competitor for his family's affections. If your dog is fully grown and firmly ensconced as a member of the family, get a kitten rather than a mature cat as a second pet.

Whichever it is, there are certain formalities to be observed when the two meet. Introduce them gradually so that each may get the scent of the other. Hold the cat or the kitten and let the dog sniff around him. Be sure to trim the cat's claws to forestall possible injury to the dog's eyes in the event of an unforeseen spat. Pay generous attention to the dog, for jealousy more than anything else instigates a pugnacious attitude in a pet dog. And, of course, avoid leaving the two alone together during the first few weeks of their acquaintance.

# 4

# The Four- to Nine-Month-Old Kitten

Up to the age of three or four months, the kitten has been very much waited on, not because constant attention is necessary, but because the owner has grown so attached to his pet by this time that he enjoys attending to his every need, real or imagined.

The period from four to nine months is the really big deal in every cat's life. So much happens! Nothing is as it used to be or ever will be again. Nature now proffers the gift of an entire set of new teeth. Once this milestone is passed and the second teeth are in and properly attended to, maturity is just around the corner.

As compared with the roly-poly kitten of the previous period, the growing kitten's appearance now leaves something to be desired. Growth up to this time has been rapid, with around one pound added to the weight every month up to six months of age. Growth now slackens off a bit. The kitten may appear lean because of increase in the size of the bony structure and loss of baby fat. Further-

31

more, the increasing degree of intelligence, so noticeable during this growing period, prompts the kitten to indulge in a few misdemeanors that warrant correction lest they become bad habits. But more about this later.

## FEEDING

Changes in feeding now mainly involve the amount rather than the kind of food. The four-months-old stomach can accommodate more food, this to be increased according to growth and the appetite of the individual as time goes on.

From weaning time to maturity, growing kittens experience marked physical changes and need a high-protein diet consisting of twice as much food per pound of body weight as normal adults. At age four months, they could not possibly consume this amount at one time, and for that reason it should be divided into three meals a day. A complete and balanced diet is a dry commercial meal with a canned food mixed in as a supplement. The amount to feed will usually be specified on the package. Just watch your kitten's progress and make sure his weight gain is constant.

Kittens should develop gradually but be slightly thin, not too roly-poly. Do not overfeed. The way you feed your kitten now will influence his eating patterns as an adult, so it's wise to establish sensible habits during kittenhood. By the time he reaches six months of age, he can be fed only twice a day.

## THE NEED FOR WATER

The need for drinking water is sometimes overlooked on the premise that an animal so addicted to milk does not need water. Milk is not a substitute for water, however, and cats should be encouraged to drink water. It is not at all unusual for the kitten approaching maturity to lose his taste for milk in favor of meat, poultry, and fish. This is the time when kittens need water to supply the necessary liquid intake.

Water is nature's carrier of body wastes. It is a food solvent and a lubricant for eyes, joints, and tissues. No animal can exist for any length of time without it, except, of course, those vertebrates adapted to utilize the metabolic water broken down through the digestion of food.

But, you will maintain, the average cat does not like water—he is so seldom seen drinking it. All too often he would drink it if it were readily available. We proved this to our own satisfaction years ago with a ground-level drinking fountain on our lawn, which, primarily for visiting birds, we kept filled with fresh water. Much to our surprise, we found the neighbors' dogs and cats drinking frequently, perhaps because no thirst-quenching provision had been made for those allowed to roam free out-of-doors.

In attempting to find out why some cats did not seem to like water, we filled a double-sided drinking dish: one side with ice water, the other with cool water. The cats sniffed both and turned away. When we filled one pan with tepid water, they drank it as if they enjoyed it. Thereafter, each morning we filled a container with ordinary tap water and left it to reach the temperature of the day. This, we learned, was the way the cats preferred it. We placed the summer outdoor fountain in the shade so it would not overheat. By this time we knew that the cats would refuse water too cold or too warm.

Whether the cat drinks much or little water, it should be made available to him as a matter of course and always in the same place so he knows where to find it.

During fevered conditions, when the body fluids are depleted, an animal naturally craves water. An unnatural urge for water, however, especially in elderly cats, may indicate diabetes you should report this at once to your veterinarian.

Water is not the same the country over: some of it is soft, some of it is hard and mineral laden. Whichever it happens to be, it rarely has any deleterious effect on the animal accustomed to it; but when he drinks strange water, he may be plagued with digestive upsets or diarrhea. When on vacation with your cat or traveling to shows, take along a supply of water from home.

### FIRST STEPS IN GROOMING

Although most cats groom themselves regularly and are very meticulous about keeping themselves clean, they require additional attention from their owners, especially if they have long hair. This is the time to begin the systematic grooming to keep your kitten's skin and coat in good condition, which will continue for the rest of his life. Grooming not only means taking care of your kitten's coat, but also his claws, ears, and eyes. The amount of grooming a cat needs depends on whether he has short or long hair. Now you should establish a regular routine, two or three times a week, for combing and brushing, and a quick check of your cat's body and condition.

Early grooming is a rather superficial business, carefully and gently done to accustom the cat to the process as well as to condition his coat. Combing and brushing are the best ways to keep your cat well groomed. Combing separates the hair; brushing spreads the natural oils through the coat, adds a gloss, and removes dead hair before it has a chance to mat near the skin. Make sure you have the proper grooming tools for a short- or longhaired coat; see Chapter 9, "Grooming," for suggestions.

Not all cats like to be combed and brushed, but most of them relish the attention they get while being groomed. Keep the sessions short at first, ten or fifteen minutes at the most, repeating them several times a week. The best place to groom your kitten is on a sturdy table, so you won't have to bend over. Don't ever place your kitten on a wobbly table; he will be frightened and try to jump off. A slippery surface can also upset him; put a rubber mat or towel on the table to give him better footing. If your kitten resents being groomed on the table, you can temporarily try to groom him when he's stretched out on your lap.

Don't give up if your first attempts at grooming are disappointing. Go slowly and be understanding. If the kitten is fidgety when you run the comb through his hair, dampen your hands and rub his entire body in the direction of the hair growth. Then brush the coat until it is completely dry and all the dead hair is removed.

The average cat does not like to be stroked the wrong way; for some reason it may irritate him to have his hair fluffed up and tousled. Accept his little idiosyncrasy, and always stroke him in the direction the hair grows. Let him lie comfortably in your lap, if he will, as you brush him from head to tail, and be especially gentle when you turn him over to brush the extra-fine fluff on the stomach. He'll soon be purring contentedly at grooming time. And as he grows older, especially when his grooming may become more time-consuming, he will enjoy the longer periods of attention.

Every time you groom your cat, be on the lookout for danger signs. Examine the skin for external parasites such as fleas, ticks, or ear mites. Part the hair and look for bald spots, scaly areas, crusts, or rashes. Look at his eyes, ears, and claws. Check around the anal opening: dried, creamy-colored segments that look like grains of rice stuck to the hair usually indicate tapeworm infestation. Turn the cat over and examine the abdomen for signs of tenderness or lumps under the skin. Your kitten will become used to being touched and will be more at ease when he has to be examined and treated by a veterinarian.

### HAIRBALLS

Hairballs are a potentially serious problem that can be forestalled to some degree by regular grooming of the coat as it is shed.

Shedding goes on practically all the time, though it is more evident in the late spring and early fall when hairs can be seen on the cat's bed or on chair coverings where he naps. The loosening of the old hair makes him uncomfortable; the cat rubs himself along the carpet in an effort to get rid of it.

In the process of licking his coat to clean the fur, the cat ingests the shedding hair. During self-grooming, the loose hair sticks to barblike backward-projecting filiform papillae on the cat's tongue. The hair is swallowed because of the backward angle of the barbs. Generally it passes through the system and is eliminated with the bowel movements. But in cats that self-groom excessively (especially longhairs that are not combed or brushed regularly), or during heavy shedding periods, the dead hair can build up inside the stomach and form into masses several inches wide that disrupt digestive functions by obstructing the bowel.

Some cats will normally cough up hairballs; but once a large mass passes from the stomach to the intestines, it cannot be regurgitated. If the mass cannot pass through the intestinal tract, constipation and other serious problems may occur. It has been estimated that hairballs are the most common cause of constipation in cats. When an intestinal impaction occurs, a cat must be treated to make the hairball pass. Treatment generally consists of an enema or mild laxative to help lubricate the mass, along with a fast of about twenty-four hours. If the hairball does not pass normally from the body, it may have to be surgically removed.

The best hairball deterrent is regular combing and brushing. The more dead coat that is removed, the less hair the cat will swallow. Keeping in mind that cats will always self-groom, however, it is advisable to use a commercial preparation to eliminate the hairballs as well as to prevent their formation. This can be purchased at any pet store. Hairball remedies are usually flavored with malt or other flavors palatable to cats. About one-quarter to one-half teaspoon is placed on the cat's nose or front paw, where it can be promptly licked off and swallowed to lubricate any accumulated hair and move it through the intestinal tract.

## TEETHING

Eruption of the second or permanent teeth usually is a painful period in a kitten's life. It begins around the fourth month and continues for several weeks as the first or milk teeth are pushed out by the permanent teeth.

The kitten's baby teeth loosen and drop out one at a time. If they loosen but do not drop out, they can often be removed by gentle pulling with the fingers. However, they may be so deeply embedded in the jawbone that the veterinarian must do any necessary extraction.

Pain caused by teething may be so severe as to induce drooling, vomiting, diarrhea, and loss of appetite. The teething period is usually short; most kittens come through it with flying colors. Throughout these few weeks, check the mouth frequently, and when the gums begin to redden and swell, give the cat safe things to chew on. These will help loosen the baby teeth as well as relieve the irritation of sore gums. *Do not give aspirin to relieve the pain of teething and sore gums unless your veterinarian specifically advises you to do so.*

## CHEWING

The tendency to chew on objects may be noticed at this age and has sometimes been wrongly termed destructiveness. To the contrary, it is the kitten's instinctive urge to help along the shedding of the temporary teeth. Articles of clothing, especially woolen sweaters, are favorites for this purpose. The chewing eases pain and pressure on the inflamed gums as the larger second teeth prepare to push out the baby teeth. The sensible answer, of course, is to keep valuable things out of reach and to substitute something that may be chewed on with impunity.

Other reasons, too, have been advanced for the unfortunate chewing habit of the four- to five-months-old pet. Irregularity in feeding is one of these. If meals are not provided at the proper time, the stomach may be empty and the kitten so hungry that he chews on whatever he can find. Feed at the same times each day and be sure that the amount fed is gradually increased with growth.

Boredom, too, is possibly to blame. The kitten that played with his brothers and sisters always had something to do; whereas as the only pet in a home, left to his own devices, he may be just plain lonely. You, the owner, are now the young cat's companion. Keep him with you as much as possible, play with him often to deepen the bond between you, and give him toys to amuse himself when he is left alone.

## TRIMMING THE CLAWS

Trimming the kitten's claws regularly will minimize the damage from clawing. Necessary as sharp claws are as a defense weapon for the outdoor cat, they are not needed for the pet that lives entirely in the home. Hence they should be shortened every few weeks. Otherwise you, as well as the judge in the showring, could be scratched once in awhile. Furthermore, untrimmed claws have been known to grow so long that they curl around and pierce (and possibly infect) the foot.

No cat likes to have his feet handled, so it is advisable to accustom your kitten to claw clipping at an early age. Scissors will not do for the job; even though they are sharp, they are not strong enough for claw trimming without frightening the kitten. You need a special cat-claw clipper that can be purchased at your local pet store.

Before attempting to clip the claws for the first time, make a practice of handling the feet every time you stroke your kitten. This will help to forestall resistance during the manicure.

The cat's claws are enclosed in sheaths. Before each one is cut, you must press on the top and bottom of the toe with your thumb and index finger to force the claw outward. It's not necessary to push hard, just the slightest pressure will push the claw out. Once the claw is unsheathed, clip off the tip. Snip off only a little at a time and by all means avoid cutting into the vein, which will make the claw bleed. If you look carefully, you can see a pink vein inside the transparent claw. Accidentally nicking the vein will cause the claw to bleed. If this happens, press a little quick-stop powder (available at most pet stores) against the claw tip for a few seconds to stop the bleeding.

### DECLAWING

Scratching, as discussed in the previous chapter, is an inherited trait of all cats. They must be trained at an early age to use a scratching post instead of your expensive household furnishings. Some youngsters have been known to bypass the post in disdain and then proceed to tear up the furniture, carpeting, or drapes. To keep your cat as a welcome family member, you may consider having him declawed as a last resort.

Declawing is a surgical procedure that involves removing the entire last joint of each toe. The toes are then sutured or bandaged tightly to keep them from hemorrhaging. The surgery requires general anesthesia and several days of hospitalization. Once the stitches or bandages are removed, the cat's feet will be rather painful for at least a week.

Declawing is a controversial procedure: cat fanciers think it is inhumane and causes behavioral changes. On the other hand, many veterinarians say that declawed cats can live normal lives without any apparent damage. Most veterinarians suggest removing only the claws on the front paws; the back ones rarely do any damage.

A declawed cat should never be allowed outdoors since he can no longer defend himself. *Never* declaw your cat impulsively. Try training him to use a scratching post first. Should problems about scratching arise, discuss them with your veterinarian.

### THE OUTDOOR LIFE VERSUS THE INDOOR LIFE

It may seem cruel to confine a cat to the house. On the contrary, it is good common sense.

The outdoor cat runs many risks. He may be lost or stolen, attacked by dogs, trapped in an enclosure, or poisoned deliberately or inadvertently when mouthing rodents that have themselves been destroyed by poison. He may be run over by an automobile. These are just a few of the countless hazards besetting the cat that explores the neighborhood unsupervised.

As far as safety and well-being are concerned, the odds seem to be in favor of keeping a cat indoors. He does not become restless about confinement, for he cannot miss what he has never had. Moreover, he can practice his favorite sport of hunting, even when house-bound, by tossing his toy mouse in the air and pouncing upon it. He might even perform a real service in country homes by discouraging any mice bent upon spending the winter in the basement or between floors. He'll give them such a lively time that they may decide to go elsewhere!

### PLAY AND EXERCISE

Play is an absolute necessity for young animals. It requires no great amount of imagination to see that it teaches the fundamentals for survival. By starting the lessons in the nest, with the mother as teacher, the young one's muscles and tendons are strengthened and thus prepared for a tooth-and-claw existence in the wild.

This principle applies to many kinds of mammals such as big and little cats, wolves, foxes, ocelots, and so on, whose play is a combination of wrestling matches, make-believe fights, biting, and clawing—in fact, all manner of give-and-take constituting attack and defense that might be encountered in later life. The cat, even more than the dog, has kept intact the natural responses inculcated by training in the wild.

Some cats kept indoors have to depend upon play as the chief source of their exercise. The principle seems to work out all right during kittenhood, but, as the years roll by, there is a tendency to avoid overactivity. In short, the well-fed, mature cat may become fat and lazy unless encouraged to exercise. Institute regular play periods including, perhaps, outdoor walks on leash. It is usual enough to meet neighbors walking their dogs on leash, but rather rare to find pet cats enjoying the same privilege.

With children in the house, the daily play periods present no problem; the kids are forever willing to oblige. They do have to be cautioned, though, to limit playtime sessions to about fifteen minutes each, two or three times daily. They have to be cautioned also against overexcitement, which can tire the kitten and growing cat, and against rough play, which may tempt the animal to nip and scratch.

# 5
# The Adult Cat

When the ninth month passes, it is reasonable to consider your cat as fully grown. Although his bony framework is now probably as large as it will ever be, the animal will round out and add a bit to his weight for the next two months. Full growth in young adult cats implies maturity to perhaps a greater degree than in varieties of other animals—dogs, for instance, whose breeds include such a wide range of sizes and physical characteristics. While most small- and medium-sized dogs reach their full height by the time they are nine months old, the large- and giant-sized breeds continue growing up to twenty months. The various cat breeds differ in coat and color but not to any great extent in size and conformation.

Regardless of breed, mature male cats generally weigh from seven to seventeen pounds, and females from six to twelve pounds. There are no giants or dwarfs among them; in fact, no effort has been made to produce specimens larger or smaller than the average. Through the years, breeders have been content to let the cat's size and natural tendencies remain the same. Once growth has been completed, domestic cats of all kinds are remarkably uniform in overall size.

### TEMPERAMENT

Only when the kitten has reached true cat's estate can we really appreciate the charm of his temperament. The kitten is much the same as any young animal. He eats, sleeps, and plays his way toward maturity, happily without imagination to plague him about the kind of life that lies ahead. The picture changes with maturity, as age provides the cloak of dignity and independence.

The mature cat is just as willing to play as the kitten, but it must be on his terms, not yours. You can ingratiate a dog but never a cat. The dog enjoys his dependence whereas the cat hates it. Many people evaluate cat temperament from what they know about dogs. Dogs are very social animals that are devoted to and dependent on their masters.

Cats are not so outwardly companionable, but they do need and enjoy attention and affection. If they do not receive it during kittenhood, they may not develop normally. Each cat is an individual and has to be handled in his own special way. Some cats are very outgoing and like being with people; others are cool and detached. They respond to a certain extent, but often not enough to let you know they are responding. There is a streak of independence in most cats that does make them rather reserved. As a rule they like people, but they do not care to be pushed into familiarity. Instead, they prefer to make the advances.

Cats are as inscrutable as the Sphinx; no one can ever say he truly knows his cat. To live and communicate with one is a unique experience.

## FEEDING

Feeding practices are basically the same as described in the previous chapter. Adult cats should be fed twice a day, preferably in the same place and at the same times each day. The amount of food required depends on the individual cat, the extent of his activity, exercise, and weight. You will be able to judge the amount of food needed to keep your cat satisfied and in good weight, neither too fat nor too thin, by observing him. If he is given more than he can manage to eat, he may nose the dish in an effort to cover it up—as if to save the oversupply for a rainy day. This is one way you can judge whether you have served too much.

If your cat eats dry food, you might like to try something called self-feeding. The cat feeds himself from a container in which dry food is always kept available. He can eat what he wants, when he wants it. When left alone, he has something to do; nibbling at his dry food may very likely take the place of nibbling on valuable household objects. Also, if you work every day and are kept away from home past the cat's regular feeding time, you know that he has food and can satisfy his hunger. An important advantage is that the blood-nutrient level is maintained more evenly. Cats that are self-fed should have unlimited access to water.

## WEIGHING

The correct amount of food, though it differs in individual cases, must be related to activity. The relaxed, luxury-loving cat needs less; the active cat needs more. Feed a basically nutritious diet to keep your cat slender and healthy. Then weigh him at frequent intervals from the one-year period on and endeavor to hold his weight at a reasonably level figure.

The average cat does not take kindly to being weighed in the usual manner. The easiest way is to take him in your arms, weigh yourself and the cat together, then subtract your own weight from the total. Particularly with the longhairs, appearance can be deceptive since the pet in full bloom may seem to have more flesh than is actually the case. So trust the scales rather than your eyes and feed accordingly.

### THE NEED FOR EXERCISE

Exercise constitutes an important phase of care for the adult cat. Feeding comes first in importance, exercise second. When a cat is fully grown, he often becomes lazy as the kittenish urge to play gradually diminishes. This applies particularly to cats that spend their entire life indoors. The cat that goes outside to an outdoor exercise run normally covers a lot of ground, whereas the homebody lolls around much of the time. Rather than cut down on the amount of food given him, the house cat should be encouraged to work it off for the ultimate good of his waistline.

When everyone in the household is out during the day, two cats can provide companionship for each other; their play periods are a form of exercise. One pet alone has little incentive to keep moving for his own good.

When there are children in the house, they will frolic constantly with their pet. Your house is an excellent exerciser as the cat can nose into every corner and run up and down stairs a dozen times a day. The apartment cat is denied these manifold pleasures that would keep him in good shape. Is it any wonder, then, that he often grows soft and pudgy?

The remedy is obvious. The house-bound cat can be given a daily walk around the block. Cats aren't easily trained to walk on leash; but if they become accustomed to wearing a collar or harness at an early age, they will adapt to it. Walking a cat on leash is nothing new. The Egyptians started it thousands of years ago. It is high time we followed their example (see page 107).

In moderate weather the well-trained cat can be given a short stroll on leash at any time of day. It is not sensible, however, to engage him in strenuous play immediately after eating or to walk him any distance at such a time.

A reasonable amount of cold in winter need not keep him from enjoying his usual stroll, for his coat at this season of the year is at its thickest. When he comes in from a walk, dry him off carefully, especially between the toes, and examine the toe pads for the slightest abrasion. His feet are not as tough as a dog's feet; they need to be inspected.

### BUILDING AN OUTDOOR RUN

When lack of time makes it difficult to exercise your cat, you can build an outdoor run if you have a backyard. The run should be as roomy as possible, with a shelter (raised off the ground) that is large enough for your cat to sleep in or crawl into during a sudden shower, and several perches on which he can sit in the sun or shade.

Outdoor runs for cats generally are constructed with wooden frames and covered with wire mesh that cannot be spread apart. The top of the run should also be covered to prevent the cat from escaping. When the weather is clear and the temperature moderate, you can leave the cat outside for several hours to enjoy himself climbing up the wire and rolling in the grass.

## THE FEMALE'S FIRST HEAT PERIOD

If your cat is a female and has not been spayed, an important concern at this age will be safety during her first heat. The average female comes in season between seven and nine months of age, depending on the time of year and the breed.

Unlike female dogs, which go into heat semiannually, female cats are polyestrous animals, which means they may experience many heat periods over the course of a year. A heat period lasts about four to seven days if the female is bred. If she is not bred, the heat lasts longer and recurs at regular intervals. Thus, a female can be in heat many times a year.

When the female is in heat, she will rub and roll around the floor and cry endlessly, looking for males to breed her. Besides being noisy and annoying when she is in heat, she often neglects to use her litter box. If you do not intend to breed your female after she reaches sexual maturity, you should consider having her spayed (see page 175).

## THE ADULT MALE

A male cat usually becomes sexually mature between nine and twelve months of age, and the habits of the adult tom often become very apparent and annoying. He may start to back up to vertical surfaces—such as chairs, drapes, and walls—and spray them with pungent-smelling urine that can make your home reek. The strong odor is supposed to "mark" his territory and to entice female cats. The tom will also become very vocal and aggressive when he wants a female. He'll want to go outdoors constantly and, if permitted to do so, will fight with other tomcats and may be seriously injured. If you do not want to breed your male, consider having him neutered (see page 175).

# 6
# The Old Cat

The cat is one of the longest lived of the smaller domestic animals. The average life span ranges from twelve to sixteen years. Many cats live much longer; the teeth of some have been observed as sound and complete for almost twenty years. The cat believed to be the oldest, known as "Ma"—a female tabby from Devon, England—died on November 5, 1957, at the ripe old age of thirty-four years and five months.

These and other exceptions, no doubt, are cats that have been given extra care and good nutrition. What is equally important, they have been blessed, in all probability, with a heredity of long-lived parents or parents with especially good teeth.

Most cats can be happy and comfortable in old age if they receive the proper care from their owners. As cats grow old, their bodies go through natural aging processes. There is a slowing up in every way, usually so gradual we hardly notice these changes taking place. Much as we regret the effects of old age, we have to accept them. It is best to know what to expect so we can be ready to deal with things.

We cannot outwit old age, but we can help prolong

an old and devoted cat's life if we recognize and deal with his infirmities before they have actually incapacitated him. Regular examination by the veterinarian, at least every six months, will go far to reducing to a minimum the ravages of the years. Periodic checkups are important for cats of all ages, but they are especially critical for aging felines. Your vet knows what to look for; he can read signs that your untrained eyes cannot.

### HOW CATS AGE

We used to think that one human year was approximately equal to seven years of a cat or dog. This analysis has been adjusted within the past ten years, as shown in the following comparison from the Gaines Research Center:

| Pet's Age | Man's Age |
|-----------|-----------|
| 6 months | 10 years |
| 8 months | 13 years |
| 12 months | 15 years |
| 2 years | 24 years |
| 4 years | 32 years |
| 6 years | 40 years |
| 8 years | 48 years |
| 10 years | 56 years |
| 12 years | 64 years |
| 14 years | 72 years |
| 16 years | 80 years |
| 18 years | 88 years |
| 20 years | 96 years |
| 21 years | 100 years |

The development of a six-month-old kitten can be compared with that of a ten-year-old child; the year-old cat with the youth of fifteen. After two years, the cat's aging slows, and each single year compares to about four human years.

## CHANGES IN THE OLDER CAT

Cats generally begin to show their age at about eight years. The aging process varies with each individual, although certain changes are obvious in all cats. The most apparent change probably will be a decline in activity. The elderly cat does not jump and run in play as he used to do; he is no longer capable of sustained exertion, and he may tire even after moderate exercise. He'll want to sleep more and may be short-tempered about things he once put up with. He cannot adjust easily to extremes of heat and cold.

The aging cat's skin glands will become sluggish. The facial hair grays, and the coat thins and loses its luxuriance. The cat may start to lose some of his hearing and sight. Problems in the mouth can develop from loose or decaying teeth, tartar buildup around the teeth and gum edges, or gum disease, making it difficult and painful for the cat to eat. If he mouths food as if it hurts him to chew, have his teeth checked by the veterinarian, and scaled or extracted as the case warrants.

The body metabolism diminishes, and the cat's vital organs begin to function less efficiently. Heart problems may occur, and kidney function may become greatly reduced. The most common type of cancer found in elderly cats is lymphosarcoma, a disease associated with the feline leukemia virus. Other problems old cats frequently experience are constipation, arthritis, diabetes, skin tumors, mammary tumors (in unspayed females), respiratory problems, digestive disturbances, liver disease, and urinary tract obstructions.

### CARING FOR THE OLDER CAT

Apart from following your veterinarian's advice, the care of an old cat consists of common sense, close observation, and lots of patience and affection.

Do not dismiss his lethargy by calling him a lazy old thing! An old cat's heart is not so strong, and endurance for him is a thing of the past. He needs less exercise and more rest.

Keep him warmer in winter and cooler in summer, for he now feels the cold and the heat as never before. Make his bed a little softer. If his favorite napping site is a chair of ordinary height, place close beside it a footstool to serve as a step-up; his joints may be stiff and painful. If your cat is accustomed to sleeping nights on the bed beside you, he will need some kind of step-up here, too. Otherwise he must be lifted up and down. A stiff-legged old cat grows very cautious about jumping either way. He doesn't want to change his sleeping habits, and he may be seen looking longingly beside the bed whose height he cannot negotiate. Once there, he is not likely to fall off, for he sleeps utterly relaxed and usually curls himself up in a ball. In addition to his nighttime rest of several hours, an old cat needs little naps during the day. There are doubtless a half-dozen cubbyholes about your house into which he can crawl for his periodic siestas. One old tabby of our acquaintance preferred to nap inside a big bookcase, behind the books where it was dark and warm and free of drafts.

An old cat often becomes less meticulous about his

toilet habits. A second litter box may be necessary in a large house. Try to be compassionate if you occasionally find some droppings beside, rather than in, the litter box: his sense of balance may be diminishing. Newspapers can be placed under the tray. Many old cats suffer from constipation. Some others become incontinent or lose the ability to control the urge to urinate or defecate. This is a serious and unpleasant problem that you should discuss with your veterinarian.

Groom your old cat often. He'll like it, and combing and brushing will stimulate his sluggish skin glands and give his coat a healthier appearance. An old cat may not be able to keep himself as clean as he used to, and a little extra grooming and sponging from you will help to maintain his dignity.

## FEEDING

Good nutrition is crucial. The dietary needs of old cats differ from those of younger cats. Seek your veterinarian's advice, for great progress has been made in the field of nutrition for geriatric cats. You might try feeding more often and serving less at each meal. If the old fellow has been accustomed to one meal daily, change to two meals; if he has had two feedings per day, now give him three—in smaller amounts, of course.

He may be picky in his manner of eating; he may develop likes and dislikes that never occurred to him before, or, if they did, you ignored them lest you spoil him. As age begins to slow him down, his sense of taste and smell begin to diminish. In such a case, topping his regular ration with a few morsels of some favorite food will make things more appealing. He's been your good companion these many years, so don't hesitate to spoil him now. He deserves it.

Some cats tend to put on weight in old age, and a few become obese. Obesity imposes a strain on the heart and can shorten a cat's life; it is very important to modify his diet if your cat is gaining too much weight. More often, though, an old cat begins to lose weight; you may notice that his spine and ribs are thinly covered with flesh.

Plenty of fresh drinking water should always be available. Cats with chronic nephritis or impaired kidney function need to drink more water than usual to expedite the elimination of waste products.

### WHEN THE END COMES

There comes a time when the penalties of age pile up and nothing remains but to put the sufferer to sleep. Euthanasia, as practiced today, does exactly that. "Euthanasia" comes from the Greek word meaning gentle and easy death, and it can be the final tribute a loving owner can give to a cat that can no longer enjoy life or is terminally ill.

Let your veterinarian decide when the time has come to say good-bye—he can decide better than you for his decision will be made medically rather than emotionally. When that time comes, the veterinarian will give him an injection. The cat literally goes to sleep before the lethal dose takes effect. When the needle is administered, there is no pain, no struggle, no knowledge of what is happening. It is all so calm and quiet that the veterinarian might allow you to hold the cat in your arms.

# 7
# Foods and Feeding

Feeding cats today is less of a chore than it has ever been before, a fact that without doubt has served as an additional incentive to an ever-growing number of people who keep cats as pets.

Increasing knowledge of the science of nutrition has enabled manufacturers to compound diets with correctly apportioned and balanced nutrients that cats need to maintain good health through their various life stages: kittenhood, adulthood, pregnancy and lactation, and old age. Such foods are readily available in cans and packages, moist or dry, and ready-mixed for instant feeding. The cat owner no longer need puzzle over what, when, and how much his pet requires. He merely reads the printed directions on package or can and serves the meal, confident that he has provided his pet with adequate nourishment.

## THE REQUIRED NUTRIENTS

A cat should be fed a balanced diet containing the correct proportions of proteins, carbohydrates, fats, vita-

# DAILY FOOD REQUIREMENTS OF CATS ACCORDING TO AGE

| AGE | EXPECTED WEIGHT | | DAILY CALORIE/BODY WEIGHT | | DAILY RATION | |
|---|---|---|---|---|---|---|
| | kg. | lb. | Cal./kg. | Cal./lb. | g. | oz. |
| Newborn | 0.12 | 0.26 | 380 | 172 | 30 | 1.1 |
| 5 weeks | 0.5 | 1.1 | 250 | 113 | 83 | 2.9 |
| 10 weeks | 1 | 2.2 | 200 | 91 | 133 | 4.7 |
| 20 weeks | 2 | 4.4 | 130 | 59 | 173 | 6.1 |
| 30 weeks | 3 | 6.6 | 100 | 45 | 200 | 7.1 |
| Adult male | 4.5 | 9.9 | 80 | 36 | 240 | 8.5 |
| Adult female (pregnant) | 3.5 | 7.7 | 100 | 45 | 233 | 8.2 |
| Adult female (lactating) | 2.5 | 5.5 | 250 | 113 | 416 | 14.7 |
| Neuter (male) | 4 | 8.8 | 80 | 36 | 213 | 7.5 |
| Neuter (female) | 2.5 | 5.5 | 80 | 36 | 133 | 4.7 |

Adapted from "Gaines Basic Guide to Canine Nutrition with a chapter on the Nutritional Requirements of Cats." Courtesy of the Gaines Professional Services.

mins, and minerals. These are basically the same nutrients required to sustain human life, only they are needed and used in different proportions by cats. Cats are classified as carnivores, or meat-eaters, and need a diet high in protein. However, their nutritional needs are not completely satisfied by an all-meat diet. When cats devour their prey, they instinctively eat a complete and balanced diet, consuming flesh, internal organs, muscles, fat, and bones. Such a diet contains almost all the essential nutrients necessary to sustain cats, and in the correct proportions.

The chart that follows this brief description of the essential nutrients lists the current nutritional requirements of cats.

*Protein*, found in meat, fish, poultry, eggs, cheese, and milk, is one of the most important nutrients in the cat's diet for growth and development of body tissue and for maintenance of optimum health. Often called "nature's building blocks," proteins are the nucleus of building material for the body organs, muscles, skin, coat, nails, and blood, and they also are a source of heat and energy.

Proteins are composed of smaller molecules known as amino acids, the number and sequence of which determine the protein's structure. Cats need twenty-three amino acids, all but eleven of which can be manufactured in the body. The remaining eleven are called "essential" amino acids because they must be furnished in the diet from outside sources.

*The Nutrient Requirements of Cats*, a publication of the National Academy of Sciences, advises that whole egg protein supplies virtually ideal concentrations of the amino acids required by cats. Eggs are safely nutritious, depending on the way they are prepared. The white is not digestible in raw form. It contains avidin, which couples in the intestines with biotin (one of the B-complex vitamins) to prevent its absorption. The yolk, on the other hand, may be fed raw or cooked. Cooked eggs can be given almost any way at all—boiled, scrambled, hardboiled, or poached.

Cats, incidentally, require about four times as much protein in their diet as do dogs. This is one important reason to feed them commercial cat foods. Such commercial cat foods also contain sufficient levels of *taurine,* an amino acid essential for normal feline vision. A deficiency of taurine in the diet can cause a progressive retinal degeneration of the eyes that can result in blindness.

*Carbohydrates* are food substances that supply energy for the body and provide the bulk, or fiber, necessary for proper intestinal function. The main sources of carbohydrates in food are starches, sugars, and cellulose. Although cats do not actually require carbohydrates in their diets, they can effectively utilize starches and sugars as energy sources. These are supplied in the diet chiefly by grains, vegetables, legumes (such as beans and peas), and starchy foods (such as potatoes or pasta). Cellulose provides little energy value and cannot be digested by cats. Nevertheless, it plays an important role in the diet by adding fiber, by regulating the distribution of water in the intestines, and by governing the formation of the feces.

*Fats* are concentrated sources of energy and add taste and texture to the cat's food. They also supply certain essential fatty acids necessary for healthy skin and glossy coat. Fats carry the fat-soluble vitamins—A, D, E, and K—within the body.

*Vitamins* are required by the body for appropriate growth, for reproduction, and to maintain health. They have no caloric or energy value and, because they cannot be produced in the body, must be furnished in the diet.

Vitamins are divided into two categories: the water-soluble vitamins (the B-complex group and C), and the fat-soluble vitamins (A, D, E, and K). Feeding a well-balanced diet, especially a reputable commercial food, will generally provide the necessary vitamin requirements in sufficient amounts. You should not add nutritional supplements to your cat's diet unless they are recommended by a veterinarian to correct a specific deficiency. Nutritional supplements can be beneficial, but overconsumption of certain vitamins can cause serious problems.

*Minerals* regulate the body's chemical balance and act as catalysts for a number of biological reactions. They are components of bones, soft tissues, muscle, teeth, and nerve cells. They help maintain the body's fluid balance and the movement of fluids through the cell walls. Minerals should be considered as a group, because their actions within the body are interrelated. Overconsumption of certain minerals—too much ash, for instance—has been associated with the formation of bladder stones in cats. In the narrow urethral passage of males especially, ash tends to collect as gravel that could possibly block the bladder. Supplementation without the advice of a veterinarian is not recommended.

### LIQUIDS

*Water* is an essential part of the diet, and fresh water should always be available for the cat to satisfy his normal requirements. The amount of water a cat will consume every day is affected by the volume of moisture in the food he eats (canned food contains about 75 percent water, for instance, while dry foods contain only 10 percent), and other factors, including environmental

## RECOMMENDED NUTRIENT ALLOWANCES FOR CATS
(Percentage or Amount per Kilogram of Diet, Dry Basis[a])

| NUTRIENT | UNIT | AMOUNT |
|---|---|---|
| Protein[b] | % | 28 |
| Fat[c] | % | 9 |
| Linoleic acid | % | 1 |
| Minerals | | |
|   Calcium | % | 1 |
|   Phosphorus | % | 0.8 |
|   Potassium | % | 0.3 |
|   Sodium chloride[d] | % | 0.5 |
|   Magnesium | % | 0.05 |
|   Iron | mg | 100 |
|   Copper | mg | 5 |
|   Manganese | mg | 10 |
|   Zinc[e] | mg | 30 |
|   Iodine | mg | 1 |
|   Selenium | mg | 0.1 |
| Vitamins | | |
|   Vitamin A | IU | 10,000 |
|   Vitamin D | IU | 1,000 |
|   Vitamin E[f] | IU | 80 |
|   Thiamin | mg | 5 |
|   Riboflavin | mg | 5 |
|   Pantothenic acid | mg | 10 |
|   Niacin | mg | 45 |
|   Pyridoxine | mg | 4 |
|   Folic acid | mg | 1.0 |
|   Biotin | mg | 0.05 |
|   Vitamin B-12 | mg | 0.02 |
|   Choline | mg | 2,000 |

**a**—"Dry Basis" refers to the value of all foods when measured without moisture.

Nutrient levels selected have satisfactorily maintained adult cats and have supported growth of kittens. It is probable that they would be adequate for gestation and lactation, but few studies have been conducted. Since diet processing (such as extruding or retorting) may destroy or impair the availability of some nutrients, sufficient amounts of such nutrients should be included to ensure the presence of recommended allowances at the time the diet is eaten.

b—Quality equivalent to that derived from unprocessed mammalian, avian, or fish muscle. Processing may lower protein quality and necessitate higher concentrations.

c—No requirement for fat, apart from the need for essential fatty acids and as a carrier of fat-soluble vitamins, has been demonstrated. The figure of 9 percent fat is listed only because approximately this amount is necessary to develop a diet with the necessary caloric density of dry matter. Fat does favorably influence diet palatability.

d—Since reliable individual estimates of the need for sodium and chlorine are not available, the need for both elements has been expressed as a recommended allowance for sodium chloride.

e—When cats are fed vegetable-protein-based diets, zinc requirements may be in excess of 40 ppm (Aiken *et al.*, 1977).

f—Higher levels may be necessary when large concentrations of unsaturated fats, such as in tuna oil, are included in the diet.

From *Nutrient Requirements of Cats*, Number 13, Revised 1978. National Research Council.

temperature and body temperature. A cat should have an adequate supply of fresh drinking water at all times. If access is not free, *clean, fresh* water should be offered several times a day. Drinking from the sink, the toilet bowl, or outdoor water puddles should be discouraged because it could make your cat sick.

*Milk* is actually a food and should not be regarded as a substitute for water. It is a good source of calcium, however, and contains other nutrients as well. If a cat is eating a balanced diet, milk, when it is offered at all, should be given after the daily ration has been consumed. Some cats cannot tolerate cow's milk and may develop diarrhea after drinking it. Others are able to drink goat's milk without getting diarrhea.

### WHAT TO FEED YOUR CAT

Most cats are fed either commercially prepared cat food or homemade diets. A majority of veterinarians, breeders, and cat owners find that cats do best eating well-balanced commercial cat foods. Today, an array of foods—dry, canned, and semimoist—nourish all kinds of cats. The commercial foods on your supermarket shelves are the results of years of conscientious research.

Homemade foods are often given to a cat as its exclusive diet. They can be made with the finest meats, poultry or fish, vegetables, and dairy products and be tasty to the cat, but they may not be complete and well balanced; in addition, they can be expensive and time consuming to prepare. Mixing many foods into a balanced diet—one that contains the correct proportions of protein, carbohydrates, fats, vitamins, and minerals for cats—requires a knowledge that few of us have. The chances of the average cat owner coming up with a diet as nourishing as those put out by manufacturers, who employ nutrition specialists and maintain research facilities, is indeed slim.

The great advantage of feeding commercial cat food is that it involves very little time or work; the cat enjoys his food because of the variety, and you can be sure he's getting proper nourishment. You may decide to supplement commercial rations with an occasional home-cooked meal. Cats enjoy variety in meals, unlike dogs, that are content to eat the same diet day after day.

## TYPES OF CAT FOOD

There is such a variety of cat food to choose from that you may be confused about what to feed your cat. Basically, there are three main types of cat food: dry, semimoist or soft-moist, and canned.

*Dry foods*, the most economical kind of cat food, usually are complete and balanced, and come in bite-size nuggets. They may contain cereal or grains, meat meals, poultry meal, fish meal, fats, dairy products, and vitamins and minerals. Dry foods contain about 90 percent solid foods and 10 percent moisture, and have a caloric value of about 300 to 400 calories per cup.

Dry foods are convenient to store and easy to feed to cats. But they have certain drawbacks, such as a low-fat content, and they are thought to be a contributory agent in inducing urinary tract problems, particularly feline urologic syndrome (FUS). It should be mentioned that other causes of FUS (principally viral infection) have been inferred, and possibly both diet and infection are involved in bringing it about (see page 124).

Most dry foods provide complete and balanced nutrition for cats. They can be served dry (with water on the

side), moistened with a little water or milk, or with a bit
of meat added to enhance the taste.

*Soft-moist or semimoist foods* are combinations of
meat, poultry, fish and their by-products, soybean, fats,
vitamins, and minerals. Although especially palatable to
cats, they tend to be rather expensive. Soft-moist foods
are packaged in airtight cellophane bags that do not require refrigeration. They are convenient and clean to
handle, the portions being premeasured for easy use.

Soft-moist foods contain from 70 to 75 percent food
solids and 25 percent moisture. They are complete and
balanced, and deliver about 250 calories in a three-ounce
package. Unfortunately, they contain large portions of
sugar, not only for flavor but to control the growth of bacteria. A diet that is high in sugar can lead to obesity.

*Canned food* comes in two different types. "Complete and balanced" canned foods are combinations of
meat, poultry, fish and their by-products, cereals or
grains, fats, and vitamins and minerals to make them nu-
tritionally complete. Depending on their ingredients,
most brands contain about 25 percent solid food and 75
percent water, and contain about 500 to 600 calories per
twelve-ounce can.

Canned "gourmet" foods are combinations of beef,
chicken, turkey, liver, kidney, salmon, mackerel, shrimp,
tuna, and other combinations of fish and animal foods.
Most, but not all of these extremely palatable foods, contain varying amounts and combinations of by-products,
and vitamins and minerals. They are usually packaged in
six-ounce cans that supply about 250 calories per container. Regrettably, canned food is rather expensive and,
once opened, spoils more quickly than the dry semimoist
type.

## SPECIAL FOODS

In addition, some dietary foods for heart disease, kidney, liver, or intestinal problems, and for obese cats, are available in canned and semimoist forms through your veterinarian.

## HOW MUCH TO FEED

Most cat-food packages recommend the amount to feed. It's always a good idea to follow the manufacturer's suggestions. Quantity requirements vary due to age, weight, temperament, activity level, climate, and digestive efficiency. For instance, kittens need more food than older cats; active breeds eat more than sedate ones; cats that roam free need more than those confined indoors; males eat more than females; and during pregnancy and lactation, queens need from 25 to 40 percent more food than usual.

The amounts suggested should serve as a guide and can be reduced or increased if your cat seems to be getting too much or not enough. Always rely on your veterinarian's advice on feeding problems.

## SERVING THE FOOD

There are two ways of feeding a cat: planned or portion feeding, and *ad libitum* or self-feeding.

Portion feeding means giving the cat an exact amount of food at specific times each day. Feeding at the same times every day encourages a steady appetite and regular bowel movements. And with this method, you can adjust the amount of food necessary to maintain, gain, or lose weight. Give your cat twenty minutes to one-half hour to eat, then remove the uneaten portion and wash the dish. It's wise to become familiar with your cat's eating habits. Some cats eat all their food within a few minutes, especially if other pets are nearby. Others like to linger over their food; in this case, provided the food doesn't become spoiled or invaded by flies in hot weather, there's no reason why it can't be left down for a longer time.

Self-feeding means keeping a dish of food available at all times. The cat eats what he wants, when he wants it. Dry and soft-moist foods are recommended for self-feeding; canned food spoils too easily. Regardless of what feeding method is used, remember to provide fresh drinking water at all times.

### MORE FEEDING TIPS

1. Serve your cat's food and water in appropriate bowls. There is a confusing variety of plastic, stainless steel, crockery, and porcelain feeding dishes at pet stores. The containers you use should be made of nontoxic material that is easy to clean and dry.

2. Even though cats thrive on an assortment of foods, they are creatures of habit when it comes to eating. They like to eat at the same times every day, in the same location, and from the same clean dish. They also like to eat in private, with no distractions from people or other pets.

3. Do not feed cold food to your cat; before serving, bring it to room temperature.

4. Food from partly used cans should be covered

with foil or plastic wrap and refrigerated promptly. Even though soft-moist foods require no refrigeration, when a pouch is opened, the unused portion should be sealed to keep it from becoming dry and stale.

5. Most cats enjoy table scraps and treats, but they should not constitute more than 10 percent of the total diet. Some human foods and treats are too rich and exotic for cats. They may provoke digestive disturbances as well as add extra calories.

6. Raw foods should not be fed to cats; this is how they become infected with certain parasites, primarily *Toxoplasma gondii,* which causes the disease toxoplasmosis.

7. Do not give your cat bones; they can stick in his throat or stomach, or pierce his intestinal wall.

### OBESITY

Active cats seldom become obese, but inactive pets confined indoors often get fat. Obesity can shorten a cat's life by hastening such conditions as congestive heart failure, kidney problems, diabetes mellitus, gastrointestinal problems, osteoarthritis, and skin troubles. Although obesity can result from glandular or hormonal defects, the primary cause is overeating. When more energy or calories are consumed than a cat's body can utilize, fat forms.

If your cat needs to lose weight, have him examined thoroughly by a veterinarian. If the condition is caused by overeating and not by a physical problem, the cat will have to be fed controlled portions of food to lose weight. Your veterinarian will establish a diet that will gradually reduce his weight. High-calorie table scraps and treats will have to be eliminated altogether. Weigh your cat once a week to be sure he is losing; if you don't notice results by the third week, get in touch with your veterinarian.

# 8

# Cat Anatomy

The domestic cat is a digitigrade mammal, of the order *Carnivora*, weighing from six to fifteen pounds or more, according to breed and condition (the heaviest domestic cat on record weighed a whopping forty-eight pounds), with an average life span of from twelve to fifteen years.

Mammals are warm-blooded vertebrate, with bodies more or less covered with hair, who feed their young with milk from the mother's breasts. A vertebrate is an animal that has a backbone or spinal column.

The *Carnivora* comprise an order of flesh-eating mammals including, among others, cats and dogs. They are characterized by large, projecting canine teeth or fangs, two in each jaw, designed for ripping and tearing the flesh of their captured prey. They have a hairy or furry coat, and toes provided with nails or claws.

The term *digitigrade* refers to the posture of the foot. The digitigrade foot walks and runs on its toes or digits with the heel up in the air, as opposed to the plantigrade foot that walks with the entire sole, from toes to heel, flat on the ground. Digitigrade movement is the most effective for a hunter because it combines speed with stability. It is generally supposed that the descendants of *Miacis* started life equipped with the plantigrade foot; then when they came down out of the trees and evolved as ground runners, they got up on their toes to promote speed. Thus the cat's feet adapted to a new way of life by evolution; they ran on their toes instead of climbing trees to escape their enemies and to procure their food.

Cats, with the exception of the cheetah,* were not provided with any great amount of sustained speed as ground runners. Instead, stealth and jumping ability compensated for lack of endurance in the chase. With patience unlimited, the cat stalked its prey and, at the appropriate moment, pounced upon it and brought it down. Thus, we find a cat's hind legs a bit longer than his forelegs; they are stronger, too, and as limber as a coiled spring. To appreciate this, watch a cat spring straight up from the floor onto a table or a chair.

The cat's body is longer than its approximate ten-inch height. The leg muscles are well developed, strong, flexible, and particularly fashioned for jumping and climbing. These qualities are accompanied by a remarkable degree of coordination and balance. In the event of a fall, most cats possess an instinctive body-righting reflex and can literally turn themselves in the air so they land on all four feet. But they can miscalculate and not *always* land right side up; in fact, many cats have been killed by falling from great heights.

The tail plays some part in contributing to balance,

---

*The cheetah, the fastest four-legged animal on earth, is the least catlike member of the *Felidae*. It howls and barks like a dog. Rather than stalk its prey, the cheetah captures it by running it down. Cheetahs, it is said, can accelerate to forty miles per hour within two seconds and reach speeds of more than seventy miles per hour. They can't maintain this speed for very long, though, and conquest depends on being able to get close to their prey before starting their deadly run.

although coordination is governed to a greater extent by the vestibular apparatus, a specialized sense organ of the inner ear. In most cases the tail is long, tapered, and fur-covered to its tip. A dependable indicator of mood, it swings slowly and gracefully except in anger, when its pace is considerably increased.

The toes—five on the forefeet, four on the hind feet—are thickly cushioned so a cat can move along without making a sound. Thick as they are, though, the soles are not especially tough. They are easily irritated by prolonged running on rough terrain. When nature designed the cat to stalk and pounce on his prey rather than track it down for miles, she withheld the tough-textured footpads customarily found on most running animals. But she equipped the toes with claws that are the cat's only defensive weapon.

## THE CLAWS

The cat's claws are retractile; that is, capable of being completely sheathed or extended as conditions warrant. When the cat is at rest and undisturbed, the claws are drawn back into a socket or sheath. This ensures silent stalking. When needed for climbing, fighting, or capturing prey, they are drawn forward and downward by an elastic tendon. Exposed, they are as sharp as little knives.

The claws can be extended or contracted at will. This action can be observed in nursing kittens when they knead their mother's breast as if to help stimulate the milk flow. In later life when accompanied by purring, kneading seems to furnish an emotional outlet indicating pleasure or contentment.

Nature left something out when she fashioned the cat's claws; she made them point in one direction. The perfect climbing foot of certain birds has a set of toes in front with claws for climbing up, and another set behind for coming down. That is why we see some birds descending a tree trunk head-down.

The cat's claws, strong and sharp as they may be, curve downward, like a sabre. Thus, a cat can be marooned in a treetop, afraid to come down. If he had the good sense to descend the same way he went up—that is, head up and hind feet down—he could descend safely, but he has not yet acquired that knack.

When we consider that the cat is capable of comparatively little sustained speed and not much endurance, we realize that the claws have contributed most to his survival. They are for fighting, for climbing, and for defense. Cats sharpen their claws on rough surfaces primarily to pull off the worn-out shells and make way for sharper ones. The wild cat clawed tree trunks to manicure his claws (and incidentally strengthen his muscles); today the domestic cat uses a scratching post for much the same purpose.

### THE TEETH

The cat's teeth are well equipped to do the work of grasping, holding, and breaking up food. Their unique slant, at a very slight inward angle, adds power to the grasp and the hold, almost in the nature of a lock grip.

Cats have two sets of teeth, the temporary or milk teeth (see page 174), and the permanent teeth, which erupt at about five months of age. The entire set of thirty permanent teeth—sixteen in the upper jaw and fourteen in the lower—is usually complete by eight months of age. Directly in front of each jaw are six small incisors, flanked by a large daggerlike canine tooth, one upper and one lower on each side. Then come the premolars—three on each side in the upper jaw, two in the lower—and behind them one molar on each side.

The teeth are of no great importance as a defensive weapon; for fighting, the cat depends upon his claws. But for eating they *are* important for conveying food to the mouth and for slicing it to a characteristically moderate degree. The carnassial teeth (the last huge premolar of the upper jaw and the lower molar on each side) bisect to produce a shearing action. They act together like scissor blades, slicing flesh into large pieces. Cats, incidentally, do not chew their food but swallow it in chunks.

The teeth should be inspected regularly since they are subject to tartar accumulation and, in older cats, to dental disease. Removal of tartar is a tricky business best left to the veterinarian lest the tender gums be injured in the process. Decay with or without ulceration is unusual in cats, but when it does occur, it can cause such pain that the animal refuses to eat.

Brushing the teeth at frequent intervals may help to preserve them to a good old age. Wrap a gauze square around the forefinger, and dip it in a mixture of half salt and half baking soda *slightly* moistened with water or a 3 percent solution of hydrogen peroxide. Carefully massage the teeth from gum to tip. Some cats submit willingly to this service while others do not. Started in kittenhood, it will usually be accepted without objection. Loose or broken teeth should be attended to immediately by a veterinarian.

### THE WHISKERS OR VIBRISSAE

Cats usually have from eight to twelve long, antennalike whiskers that fan out sideways on each side of the upper lip, plus a few bristles that stick out over the eyes. These function as delicate, fast-acting sensory organs. Their slightest contact with an object arouses the network of nerve endings that surround the roots implanted in the skin. When a cat creeps through restricted spaces or moves in darkness, the whiskers furnish information on the immediate environment.

### THE TONGUE

The surface of the cat's tongue is covered with barblike backward-projecting papillae that help to hold food or to clean flesh from the bones of prey. The raspy tongue projections also serve as a brush and comb. The cat uses his tongue to clean his coat and at the same time pull out loose hairs about to be shed. Persistent licking of the coat may also be an instinctive act designed to remove as much as possible of the cat's body scent so that, when stalking, he will not alert his victims to his presence.

### THE SENSE OF SMELL

The sense of smell is important in food identification, sexual determination, and territory marking. Although the cat has a keen sense of smell, he does not track prey by scent. Stealth and patience are his strong points. He prefers to sit for hours, if need be, beside a tiny hole out of which he knows by the scent that a mouse or rat will emerge sooner or later. The moment it does, he springs on it like lightning, stunning it with a blow of his paws, or biting into the nape of its neck. If the prey wiggles a bit, he is all the more delighted to tease it, let it run, catch it again, and toss it in the air. The average cat does not just kill to eat; he often plays predatory games for fun, capturing almost any small thing that moves.

Cats have another sense that is associated with smell and taste. It involves the Jacobson's or vomeronasal organ, a tiny sac linked by a duct to the roof of the mouth. The Jacobson's organ is present in cats, horses, and other mammals, but not in man. Cats make a unique facial grimace called the flehmen reaction when the Jacobson's organ is stimulated. When a cat is flehming, he opens his mouth slightly and curls his upper lip. As he inhales, he picks up traces of intriguing odors on his tongue that are transferred to the duct of the Jacobson's organ when his tongue touches the roof of the mouth. This, in turn, transmits sensations to the hypothalamus of the brain that determines the cat's reaction.

The flehmen reaction is most often observed in tomcats when they respond to sex pheromones in the urine and vaginal secretions from queens in heat, but it may also be noticed in both males and females when they react to catnip and certain other provocative odors.

**THE SENSE OF HEARING**

The cat's sense of hearing is also acute, except in a few all-white specimens that may be congenitally deaf. A normal cat, however, can detect the slightest of sounds as well as ultrasonic frequencies much higher in pitch than can be determined by the human ear. The upper ranges of human hearing ability reach about 18 to 20 kilohertz (kHz) or 18,000 to 20,000 cycles per second. The cat's hearing ranges from 20 to 60 kHz, or 20,000 to 60,000 cycles per second and possibly higher. This is about two octaves above the extent of human hearing and about half an octave higher than the extent of canine hearing.

The ears are comparatively large, pointed at the top, with open, funnel-shaped bases. The muscles of the outer flaps, or *pinnae*, allow the ears to move backward, forward, and downward in a rotating manner to detect the slightest sound.

Fine hairs within the cup of the ear screen out particles of foreign matter; even so, the ears do collect a certain amount of dust and dirt as well as an accumulation of wax. Foreign matter of any sort prompts the cat to scratch his ears and thus risk infecting them, perhaps seriously. Ear mites, such tiny parasites that you never notice them, frequently infest the ears and promote intolerable itching.

The best way to forestall ear troubles is to inspect the ears regularly, keep them clean, and regard persistent scratching as a signal for immediate action. If you find dirt or accumulations of wax, clean them out with a cotton ball dipped in warm water or a pet ear-cleaning lotion that is safe for cats. Wipe gently over the part of the ear that is visible to you. Never probe deeply into the ear; you could push the foreign matter deeper into the canal or, worse yet, cause damage.

Persistent scratching, frequent shaking of the head, tilting the head to one side, foul odors, or excessive wax build-up indicate infection or the presence of ear mites. These conditions require immediate veterinary attention.

### THE SENSE OF SIGHT

Sight has been called the cat's keenest sense. As compared with body size, the eyes are large. Placed wide apart and well to the front, their vision is binocular; that is, both eyes see an image at the same time. Their most interesting feature is without doubt their color.

All newborn kittens have blue eyes that occasionally darken with growth to a deeper shade, or they may end up at maturity an entirely different color. The variation in iris color is dazzling and includes the yellows (chartreuse yellow, golden yellow, gold, amber), the oranges (orange, copper, deep copper, hazel), the greens (chartreuse green, gooseberry green, brilliant green, emerald), and the blues (bright blue, china blue, sapphire, deep blue, violet). And white cats with one blue and one copper eye (these are called "odd-eyed") are not unusual!

The iris or colored part of the eye is a curtain designed to shield the pupil from injurious glare. In bright light it draws over the pupil until a mere vertical slit is observed in the center. In dim light, the opposite happens as the iris draws back to permit as much light as possible to enter the eye. Cats see well in dim light, but they cannot see in total darkness. Like our eyes, cats' eyes have two forms of light-sensitive cells, rods and cones, in the retina. The rods are used to see in low lighting and at night, while the cones reveal a sharper image at higher levels of illumination. A cat's eyes contain more rods and fewer cones than a human's; consequently they can see better in dim light, although they cannot perceive sharp details.

A cat's eyes appear to glow at night when light shines on them because of iridescent layers called the *tapetum lucidum* located behind the retina, which reflect and amplify the light to increase vision in semidarkness.

For years, scientists believed that cats were either totally or partially color blind, but now they know that cats can distinguish color, especially greens and blues, although not as effectively as humans can.

The eyes are a good indicator of condition. They should appear bright, clean, clear, and wide open. A bit of matter in the corners need not be considered serious, but the mucus should be removed with a soft cotton ball, slightly moistened with warm water. Never rub over the eye with the cotton, however, because you could scratch the eyeball.

Any thick discharge, or prominent appearance of the third eyelid or nictitating membrane (the thin fold of skin at the inside corner of the eye that normally is barely visible), is an indication of potential trouble. All irritations and abnormalities should be checked by a veterinarian as soon as possible.

### COAT AND SKIN

Whether long or short, the cat's coat is truly his crowning glory. It is a thing of beauty, unusual in its wide assortment of colors, which include white, black, blue, silver, red, cream, chocolate, lilac, chinchilla, tortoise-shell, and many others. Cat may be solid-colored or spotted, striped, shaded, banded, or ticked in pattern. In fact, it's almost a case of finding a cat that is any color you want!

The skin of the healthy cat is smooth and supple. Its coloring can range from pale pink or silver to brown or black. The luxurious coat provides insulation against all kinds of weather. The majority of cats have two-ply coats: a soft undercoat and a slightly coarser topcoat. In the shorthairs, the fur, though dense, lies flat; in the longhairs, it is long and fluffy.

A good coat does not just happen. Its length and texture are dictated by heredity; its density, to some degree by the season of the year and the kind of life the animal leads—that is, indoors or outdoors. And since the hair is implanted in the skin, the latter must be free of parasites and skin disease for the coat to appear at its best. In other words, a good coat cannot be expected to grow out of a poorly conditioned skin (see page 93).

Shedding occurs practically all the time, although it is more noticeable when nature is preparing the coat for the temperature of the season ahead. Serious illness, too, is accompanied by shedding, and queens drop much of their coat after weaning their kittens. The old coat, about to be cast, is apt to be lifeless and a bit faded; the new growth is bright, shining, and more accurately intense in its color.

# 9
# Grooming

People who keep one or more cats in the house often complain that "their hair gets all over the place!" So it does, but only under certain conditions. Shed hair can be quite a problem that, to a great extent, can be minimized by regular grooming.

Hair on the furniture, however, is not the most significant reason for grooming. What is more important, daily grooming promotes good health; it removes the old hair as it is cast and makes way for the new growth. The coat is being constantly renewed, although a greater amount of shedding takes place normally during spring and summer when it mats the longhaired varieties and spoils the bright, sleek look of the shorthairs.

Even though the longhaired breeds need the most grooming, all cats, whether household pets or show animals, need daily attention to make them look their best and to prevent other problems from developing. If we do not groom daily or at least twice weekly and remove the loose hairs from the coat, the cat tries to do it himself because they make him uncomfortable. He may rub himself under sofas and chairs until his skin is irritated. The cat will also remove the loose hair as he washes himself.

He'll lick himself persistently with his rough-surfaced tongue that serves almost like a comb, and in the process, he gets hair in his mouth and swallows it. The swallowed hair can form into a sausage-shaped mass in the stomach and cause constipation or more serious problems. So, the more systematically we groom the coat, the less hair is ingested.

### BRUSHING AND COMBING

Start brushing and combing in kittenhood if the young one will stand for it. Some will, others will not. If done very gently, cats of all ages learn to accept grooming as a regular practice and actually enjoy it. That is the key to grooming without resistance: make it a pleasant interlude.

The kind of brush and comb you need depends on the length of your cat's coat. A natural, short-bristled brush will serve for the shorthaired breeds whereas a natural, long-bristled brush will be more effective on the longhairs. Rubber brushes are best for the kitten's first sessions and for older cats that are not accustomed to being groomed. A fine-wire slicker (an oblong brush with short, bent-wire teeth) may help to remove mats and tangles from longhaired breeds.

Select a fine-tooth, metal comb for the shorthaired breeds. Longhairs need a metal comb with two different teeth-spacings: a medium side for preliminary combing, and a fine side for thorough combing. The fine side can be used around the head and neck where the ruff looks better when standing out in windblown style. Whatever type of comb is selected, wield it gently, slowly. It is neither a rake nor a hoe but a safe tool for removing loosened hair. Only when the coarse-tooth comb goes through the coat without interference is it advisable to use the fine-tooth comb to separate further and remove the hair about to be cast.

Try to begin the first grooming sessions when your cat is relaxed and just a trifle sleepy. Perhaps he likes to stretch out on your bed or be cuddled in your lap. If so, begin his beauty treatment then, and hear him purr with pleasure.

First, stroke him as in ordinary petting, then with both hands give him a thorough finger massage right down to the skin. This will help to remove the loose hair. Then proceed to brush from head to tail, in the direction of the hair growth. And do be extra gentle when going over the stomach where the skin is very tender. Brushing helps to loosen the dead hair and to add a sheen to the coat, but combing is more important to remove all the loose, dead hair.

On shorthairs, you want to comb the hair from head to tail, in the same direction that you brushed. On long-hairs, place the teeth of the comb down to the skin and comb upward, to lift out all the dead hair and to straighten the undercoat. If there are any mats or tangles, try to pull them apart with your fingers, carefully separating them into smaller sections. Then, as each section is separated, carefully comb it. If the coat has become one solid mass to the skin, a professional groomer may have to clip the hair off with an electric clipper. Although that may sound unkind, clipping is more humane than agonizingly tugging out large clumps of mats. Don't fret: the hair will grow back in a few weeks, and clipping often makes the hair grow in thicker.

### BATHING

Cats that are groomed regularly seldom need bathing. If the coat becomes soiled with dirt, grease, urine, or feces, however, you will need to clean it. And occasionally there are medical reasons for bathing, such as when an insecticidal shampoo is necessary to rid the cat of fleas, or a medicated shampoo must be given to help clear up certain skin disorders.

The kitchen sink, the bathroom sink, or a laundry tub in a warm utility room are good places to bathe your cat. Before you begin, make sure the room is draft-free, and that all the windows and doors are closed. It is also preferable to have someone assist you if possible.

Assemble all the necessary supplies ahead of time: a flexible shower spray that attaches to the faucet, or a couple of plastic bowls for wetting and rinsing, a washcloth for cleaning the face, shampoo, and a few towels. If you plan to fluff dry your cat's hair, you'll also need a hair dryer and a clean brush and comb. Cats become frightened when they stand on slippery surfaces, so it helps to place a rubber mat or towel in the sink to keep them from slipping.

Your cat should be thoroughly brushed and combed before the bath. Place a little cotton in each ear and, if you don't use a tearless shampoo, drop a tiny bit of mineral oil into the corner of each eye to prevent irritation.

Stand the cat in the tub and wet the coat all over with warm water from the shower spray or the plastic bowl. Keep the spray nozzle close to the skin to help wet the hair faster. If the nozzle is held away from the body, water splashing off the coat can frighten the cat. Hold the cat firmly by the scruff of its neck.

Pour mild shampoo (formulated for cats) over the

coat and work up a lather, taking care not to get it into the eyes or the mouth. Massage the entire body, squeezing the fur as if you were washing a sweater. Wash the face and ears with the washcloth. If your cat is very dirty, rinse lightly, then shampoo a second time. Then rinse, rinse, rinse, preferably with a tepid water spray. Much of the harm done the coat by bathing stems not from the shampooing but from insufficient rinsing, since the slightest vestige of soap left in can ruin the appearance of the coat for a while.

After rinsing, squeeze the water from the coat, then wrap a towel around the cat to soak up the excess moisture. Drying is important; it must be done as quickly as possible and in a warm area so the cat does not get chilled. If you want the hair to dry naturally, confine the cat inside his carrier some distance in front of a heater. If you want to make the hair fluffy and the cat is not afraid of a hair dryer, use one on a "warm" setting. As the nozzle blows on the hair, brush or comb, using short, quick strokes on shorthairs, and long, sweeping strokes on longhairs.

### ALTERNATIVE WAYS OF CLEANING THE COAT

If your cat absolutely detests a bath or is ill, pregnant, or old, you can use dry or no-rinse shampoos formulated for cats as alternatives. Such nontoxic products are sold in pet stores in powder, foam, or liquid form and are very effective provided your cat is not too dirty.

Stand your cat on a towel or sheet of paper. When using a dry shampoo, sift the powder into the hair, leave it on for a few minutes to absorb the dirt and oils, then brush it out. When using foam or liquid no-rinse shampoos, apply the product to the hair, work up a lather, then towel dry.

### STUD TAIL

This is a condition that is characterized by a greasy accumulation at the base of the tail, usually with crust formation on the skin. It occurs when the numerous sebaceous glands on the upper surface of the tail secrete a dark, waxy substance that discolors the hair and often smells bad. Although stud tail occurs most often in breeding toms, it is seen in females and neutered males as well.

The greasy secretion should be spot-cleaned frequently. Regular shampoo may not remove the grease, and you may have to resort to a liquid dish detergent or waterless hand cleaner (rub the cleaner into the fur and it will become a clear liquid.). Rinse thoroughly to remove all traces of hand cleaner or detergent from the coat. Do not apply detergent or hand cleaner and leave your cat unsupervised; he may lick his coat and ingest the product.

### EXTERNAL PARASITES

External parasites are organisms that live on the skin and often feed off the cat's blood. They are extremely debilitating; a heavy infestation of bloodsucking parasites can cause anemia. If your cat suddenly starts biting or licking his coat frantically, or if you see reddened skin or patches of hair falling out, he may be infested with parasites and steps to eradicate them should begin immediately. To save your cat a great deal of discomfort, check the skin and coat regularly during grooming sessions.

## FLEAS

Cat fleas, or *Ctenocephalides felis*, are the most common external parasites. They will readily infest dogs and people as well as cats; in fact, experts say that cat fleas are by far the most prevalent species found on cats and dogs today.

Adult fleas are tiny, dark brown, wingless insects with piercing mouths. They bite the host animal and suck its blood. Fleas are difficult to spot because they move quickly. As you go over the coat, you may see a small, dark bug scurrying through the fur; and if you find clusters of small black specks that look like coal dust on the skin, you may be sure fleas are somewhere in the vicinity.

Fleas should be eradicated at once for several important reasons:

1.  Their bites are extremely irritating and cause the cat to scratch frantically. *Flea Allergy Dermatitis*, a common skin disease in cats, is caused by a hypersensitivity to flea bites. It is characterized by intense itching, acute moist dermatitis, and the formation of small crusty lesions on the lower back near the base of the tail and on the inside surfaces of the hind legs. The allergic agent is found in the saliva of fleas and injected into the cat when the fleas bite. Some cats are so sensitive that they will break out from the bite of just one flea. This condition must be treated by a veterinarian.

2.  Fleas are the intermediate host for a species of cat tapeworm. A cat infected with tapeworm will often pass flat, creamy, egg-filled segments

in the stool. If the eggs are eaten by fleas, they complete the larval stage of their life inside the fleas. Thereafter, should even one infected flea be swallowed by another cat during the process of self-grooming, the tapeworm larvae migrate to his intestines where they become attached to the intestinal wall and grow into adult worms.

3. Fleas also carry several viral, bacterial, and blood-borne diseases. The microscopic parasite *Hemobartonella felis*, which causes feline infectious anemia, can be transmitted by fleas and other bloodsucking parasites.

### CONTROLLING FLEAS

Ridding a cat of fleas involves two separate courses of action: (1) killing the fleas on the cat's body by the use of insecticidal shampoos, sprays, powders, or flea collars; and (2) killing the fleas and eggs in the cat's environment.

Many insecticidal shampoos, sprays, and powders are available from your veterinarian or pet shop. Just be sure that the phrase "for use on cats" appears on the label. Follow directions *carefully*, because the cat could be poisoned by licking off or absorbing too much insecticide. A flea collar should be removed from its sealed pouch and aired for about twenty-four hours before it is placed around the cat's neck. Check the neck every day for the first week or so to make sure there is no hypersensitivity. If you own more than one pet, each one should receive this attention.

After you have treated your cat, you should thoroughly vacuum or clean all the carpets, floors, baseboards, cracks, and crevices in your house where flea eggs may hatch. Wash the cat's bedding thoroughly. If this is not possible, destroy it and provide new bedding. If you have a heavy infestation, use a household fogger or hire a professional exterminator. If you put off or neglect treating the surroundings, your cat will quickly become reinfested.

### LICE

Lice are less of a problem for the simple reason that so few cats have them. Occasionally, however, they do infest cats; and since they cling so closely to the skin, their presence often goes unnoticed. In any appreciable numbers, lice can endanger the health of a cat because they suck his blood.

Easily recognized by their bluish gray color, lice can be removed with a comb, but their tiny silver-colored eggs are difficult to dislodge. As a rule they can be killed by the application of insecticidal shampoos and dips formulated to remove fleas and ticks on cats.

### TICKS

Ticks are the hardiest of the bloodsucking parasites. They hide in warm, moist areas and attach themselves to passing animals.

Ticks attach themselves firmly by their mouths. When they bite, they force their fishhook-shaped mouths into the skin and suck the cat's blood. This not only lowers the animal's resistance to disease (eventually causing anemia in heavy infestations), but it causes intense itching and scratching that often results in secondary skin infections.

As a tick sucks blood, it grows in size. To anyone not

familiar with ticks, an engorged one may look like a small taupe-colored skin tumor. As soon as you see ticks, they should be removed. Merely pulling them off, however, often causes the head to stay embedded in the skin, resulting in an infection. Instead, you should douse the ticks with alcohol or an insecticidal spray to help paralyze them and loosen their grip. Then grasp each one with tweezers and pull it straight out. If you don't use tweezers, protect your fingers with a piece of paper. Once each tick is pulled out, swab the area with an antiseptic. Flea/tick shampoos, sprays, and collars also help to control infestation.

### EAR MITES

Ear mites, or *Otodectes cynotis*, are irritating pests that live in a cat's ears. Ear mites can be spread to young kittens from their mothers and also can be passed among all the cats and dogs in a household. Ear mites pierce the skin to feed on lymph and serum. Like fleas, they inject saliva into the skin, which causes intense itching and scratching. Affected cats will claw at their ears or shake their heads violently, often causing a great deal of damage. The frenzied clawing or shaking sometimes produces a blood blister or hematoma in the ear flap.

Although ear mites usually are not visible to the naked eye, they can be seen with a magnifying glass. You can suspect their presence if your cat shakes his head and scratches at his ears, if your cat has sores around the edges of his ears, or if you notice a lot of dark brown wax inside the ears. Your veterinarian can prescribe a feline-approved insecticide to kill ear mites.

## SKIN DISEASES

Although cats have fewer skin problems than dogs or people do, they can experience a variety of dermatological disorders. When in normally good condition, the cat's skin is elastic. When you grasp it over the back, then let it go, it springs right back to its tight fit. In most cats, the skin is normally pale pink in color; in a few others, it is dark or spotted.

The most common trouble sign is scratching, perhaps followed by the appearance of lesions, and a breaking out of blisters or bumps on the surface of the skin. Often, the cat's frenzied scratching and biting to gain relief aggravates the condition.

It's best to consult with your veterinarian at the first sign of any problem involving the skin. The quicker these conditions are diagnosed and treated, the better the chance of curing them.

### ECZEMA

Eczema is a troublesome condition that can be caused by allergies, nutritional deficiencies, parasitic infections, hormone imbalance, and grooming neglect.

The condition manifests itself in two forms: dry and moist. In the dry form, the skin becomes scaly with cracked and inflamed spots. In the moist form, red, ulcerated spots appear on the skin. In most cases, the affected areas are made worse by the cat's biting, scratching, and licking to gain relief. And these actions can quickly cause a relatively minor condition to mushroom into a serious one. If untreated, eczema can cause untold misery for your cat.

The best way to deal with eczema is to prevent the initial irritation by maintaining a regular brushing schedule to remove dead hair and dirt and to keep the skin clean, by keeping the cat and his environment free of external parasites, and by being on the lookout for any signs of trouble, especially the cat's licking of certain areas. A number of products provide temporary relief, but most stubborn cases of eczema must be treated internally.

### MANGE

Mange is a term describing skin and coat damage caused by several types of parasites.

*Sarcoptic Mange*, or scabies, caused by the feline sarcoptic mange mite *(Notoedres cati)*, is an extremely contagious condition. The mites live on and burrow into the skin causing it to thicken and become inflamed and intensely itchy. It frequently starts on the ear tips, spreads to the face, eyelids, and neck, and can extend to the feet. Diagnosis is confirmed by microscopic examination of deep skin scrapings. Treatment generally involves the use of medicated baths, followed by insecticidal dips. Since sarcoptic mange is highly contagious, all pets in the family should be treated at the same time.

*Demodectic* or "red" mange is caused by the demodectic mange mite *(Demodex cati)*, which lives in the hair follicles. The skin reddens, the hair falls out, and the follicles become infected, sometimes oozing pus and blood. Infections in cats usually start on the eyelids and areas around the eyes.

Diagnosis involves microscopic examination of the hair roots and skin scrapings. The condition is usually treated by medicated baths or dips and possibly oral medication or injections.

*Cheyletiella*, also called "walking dandruff," is caused by the cheyletiella mite, a large parasite that lives on the skin. It is a very unsightly condition characterized by mild itching and an abundance of yellowy gray scales that resemble dandruff. Treatment involves a thorough cleansing with an antiseborrheic shampoo to remove the scales, followed by insecticidal dips at intervals that depend on the product used.

## RINGWORM

Ringworm is caused by a fungus that, like mange, can be identified only under a microscope or by culturing. The disease takes its name from the circular-shaped affected areas. It may first appear as round or irregular rough and scaly patches on the cat's head, raised above the normal level of the skin. Some lesions can barely be seen while others may be scaly or crusted formations that discharge pus. If the disease goes untreated, it spreads rapidly over the body, and the cat's licking and scratching can cause bacterial infection. Treatment involves shaving off the infected hair, the application of fungicidal and fungistatic ointments, plus oral doses of the drug Griseofulvin. Griseofulvin should not be given to pregnant queens, however, since it is known to cause birth defects.

Ringworm can be transmitted from animal to animal and from animal to man. Wear gloves when handling an affected cat, and wash your hands thoroughly with antibacterial soap before touching any parts of your body. Infected animals should be isolated from contact with people and other pets. It is also necessary to sterilize or destroy the cat's bedding, collars, and other contaminated articles.

### FELINE ACNE

Feline acne is a condition that affects a cat's chin and the edges of the lips. In the early stages, it is characterized by dark specks that look like blackheads; if the condition is neglected, pustules often form, and the entire chin may become infected. This condition seems to occur when dirt or food particles clog the pores. Your veterinarian can recommend an antibacterial shampoo to clear up the irritation and also prescribe an oral antibiotic.

# 10
# Behavior and Training

If you expect to live with your cat in perfect harmony, it is important to understand his natural instincts and behavior patterns that have developed through the years. Like his wild relatives, the domestic cat is naturally inclined to be a loner, to hunt for his prey, to mark his territory and defend it vigorously, and to communicate his feelings by certain body signals and vocalizations.

## PREDATORY BEHAVIOR

A cat's predatory training begins in the nest. Kittens chase, stalk, and pounce on each other. Their movements are awkward at first, but soon the kittens learn a great deal about hunting. Although predatory behavior is largely instinctive, it can also be affected by early experiences. Queens that are allowed to go outdoors may bring killed prey for the kittens to eat. Later, the kittens may accompany their mother on a hunting trip. The rivalry between a kitten and his littermates or mother to be the first to catch and kill prey often determines whether the youngsters will grow up to be good hunters. If kittens are denied these early experiences, they are less likely to become real predators.

Most domestic cats are intrigued by anything that moves but usually do not attack anything larger than themselves. They generally prey upon mice, rats, squirrels, moles, and other small animals—flies, butterflies, grasshoppers, crickets, frogs, toads, lizards, and birds—which they eat or carry back home to present to their owners.

Both wild cats and domestic house pets follow an established ritual when hunting. When a victim is located, the cat silently stalks it, and then approaches it by swiftly running forward with his stomach held close to the ground. This sequence may be repeated several times until the cat comes within striking distance. When he gets close to the prey, he will hide under cover and assume a watching position with his body flat against the ground and his whiskers spread out. The cat then prepares for his final assault. His hind legs move backward and he begins to tread up and down; his hindquarters raise up and sway from side to side, and his tail begins to twitch.

When the cat attacks, he springs forward and pounces on his victim. His front claws hold the prey as he bites into the nape of its neck. The combination of the cat's powerful jaws and daggerlike teeth sever the victim's spinal cord and death usually is instantaneous. Sometimes a cat will release the prey, then grab and shake it several times before making the final kill.

### TERRITORY

As predators, cats select and establish their territory, which they do not like to share with others of the same species. They will defend their territory, when necessary, from other cats and mark its boundaries.

Domestic cats, particularly those that live in urban areas, don't always choose their own territories; they are often forced to share space, and they do so because they rely more on their owners than on hunting for their food. However, each cat will have a private home base— favorite spots for sleeping, observation, playing, sunbathing. Its range depends on the cat's age and sex. Most females and neuters are quite content with a limited area of their home or garden, while tomcats will protect a larger territory. The boundaries of a cat's territory are fixed. Within them, an intruder must be prepared to confront the resident cat; outside them, he will be overlooked.

Beyond a cat's private territory are common meeting places where local cats congregate for activities such as hunting, courting, and fighting. To reach them, cats use a number of private and common thoroughfares. Here neighborhood cats are tolerated in a way that strangers are not.

### MARKING COMMUNICATION

Smell is one of the most important of a cat's senses. Cats can smell things that people can't detect. Scent also plays a vital role in territory marking and sexual identification. Once cats claim their territory, they mark it with their personal scent. The ritual of scent marking defines the boundaries of the territory and reveals the cat's presence to other animals. Cats mark their territories by spraying urine, by scratching wood, and by rubbing.

· *Urine spraying* is done principally by tomcats (unneutered males), although the practice is occasionally seen in females and neuters. Tomcats mark the boundaries of their territory by spraying objects such as trees, shrubs, fences, walls, and so forth. The cat first examines the object, then turns his back to it. He holds his tail erect, twitches, then sprays a stream of urine at a height convenient for other cats to sniff. The urine contains hormonal substances known as pheromones that reveal the tom's presence to other cats in the area. When another male wanders into the area, he can tell by smelling how recently the marking occurred. Spraying usually increases during mating season, when the strong-smelling odor of a tomcat's urine tells females that he is available for breeding.

*Scratching wood*—tree trunks, for instance—is another type of marking behavior that leaves visual as well as olfactory signs; it also identifies the cat's territory. Tomcats often make these motions after they have sprayed the object with their urine.

The cat will scratch a vertical or horizontal piece of wood or a tree trunk with his front paws. He does this by extending his forelegs, pushing his claws out of their sheaths, and drawing them downward on the roughened surface. This action not only conditions the extension and retraction of his front claws but also helps to remove their loose and frayed outer sheaths. (Cats use their teeth to remove the loose sheaths on the hind paws.) As well as leaving a visible signal, secretions from the sweat glands on the paw pads mark the scratched area with the cat's scent.

Many indoor cats, regrettably, will engage in a form of territory marking in their owners' homes and ruin furniture, carpets, drapes, doors, and walls. New objects as well as old favorites are repeatedly clawed, and the longer an article is scratched, the harder the habit is to break. This behavior is seen most often in cats that have little or no opportunity to scratch trees outdoors or scratching posts indoors.

*Rubbing* is the third type of marking behavior. Cats have many sebaceous glands around the lips, on the chin, on the sides of the forehead, and along the tail. These glands are located in places that cats like to rub, and such behavior is a form of marking inanimate objects, favorite individuals, and other animals. As a cat rubs a person or an object, he deposits a sebaceous scent that can be detected by other cats.

### HOW CATS COMMUNICATE

Cats have a highly developed communication system and use various parts of their bodies as well as their voices to express their feelings. They will indicate in very specific ways if they are contented or aggravated.

A cat's ears and eyes are important mood indicators. When a cat is contented, his ears will be erect. The ears of an angry cat will flatten sideways, the pupils of his eyes will dilate, his mouth will open, and he will make hissing or spitting sounds. The tail will also tell you something about a cat's mood. A happy and contented cat gently waves his tail from side to side. A tail held very straight and high can be a kind of greeting or a sign of pleasure in being stroked. The cat that lashes his tail from side to side, however, or thumps it on the ground, is angry. A frightened cat will puff out each hair until his tail becomes more than twice its normal size. Skepticism may make only the hair near the base of the tail rise.

Various body positions can tell humans or other cats whether they can come nearer. Contentment or relaxation is expressed in several ways, such as when a cat lies stretched out on one side or rolls himself tightly in a ball and is totally oblivious to what's going on around him. An aggressive cat uses body language to intimidate his opponent. He faces his enemy head on, making direct eye contact, poised to strike. His ears are pulled back; his mouth is wide open, lips curling in a snarl as he hisses and screams. By contrast, the characteristic Halloween cat profile—legs erect, back arched, bristling tail held to one side—is a defensive stance taken in the face of aggressive behavior from another animal.

Cats also use a number of different sounds to express contentment, bewilderment, anger, aggression, pain, and other reactions. These are categorized as murmurs, vowels, and strained-intensity sounds, and include purring, meowing, snarling, hissing, spitting, screaming, and the high-pitched mating call. Some breeds—especially the Siamese—are more talkative than others.

### CATS AND CATNIP

Catnip or catmint (*Nepeta cataria*) is exceptionally stimulating to most cats. They like to sniff at the plant, lick or chew the leaves, or rub their heads and roll in it until they become almost intoxicated with its aroma. In fact, both male and female cats assume many of the postures used by queens in heat, such as rolling on the ground and treading, as well as the flehmen reaction. The scent of catnip may stimulate cats because it contains *nepetalactone*, a substance that is said to resemble closely a chemical that appears in the urine of tomcats.

More than two-thirds of all cats respond to catnip in degrees varying from high to low intensity, while the rest do not respond at all. The response seems to be inherited, and those that have a high-intensity reaction pass into an almost psychedelic state that lasts from five to fifteen minutes. The effects are harmless, however, and not habit forming.

Its popularity has induced manufacturers to add catnip leaves to stuffed cat toys. You can also purchase catnip extract at most pet stores; it can be sprayed on scratching posts to make them more appealing.

## YOU CAN TRAIN YOUR CAT

Cats often become mischievous and destructive because their owners believe they can't be trained or disciplined. But cats *can* be trained and disciplined, and the best time to start is as soon as your kitten moves into your home, before bad behavior patterns have a chance to develop. Young cats learn easily and quickly. Their brains mature just as quickly as their bodies, and by six months of age, they are well on their way to being physically and intellectually developed.

## NAMING YOUR CAT

The first step in training your cat is to name him. An adult cat will already have a name to which he responds, and it is best for the cat not to change it. But you can select a name for a young kitten, even though his registration paper (if he is a purebred) bears a name the breeder selected for him.

Choose a name for the kitten the moment you bring him home. Once you have found the right name, use it as soon as possible. Does it sound too much like another word you use often? That may confuse your cat and slow down his training. Perhaps you should choose something unique. If the name you like is very long, try to abbreviate it into a shorter call name. "The Great Mister Thomas" may be an adorable title, for instance, but quite a hodgepodge of sounds for the kitten to associate with himself and to respond to. You might pick "Thomas" or "Tommy" as his short call name.

Use the cat's name at every opportunity. He will soon understand that the name is his and his alone, and he will respond to it even if no more than to look up at you. And the cat that responds to his name is ready to be trained. Whenever you speak to him, preface your remarks with his name. *"Thomas, come!"* will evoke more certain response than the order alone.

### "COME!"

The next lesson is to train your cat to come when called. Cats are often thought to be untrainable because they are so independent and distant. You can train your cat to respond to certain vocal commands, however, by taking advantage of his natural habits and by offering rewards. It's not difficult to establish good behavior if training begins during kittenhood and is consistent.

The best way to start training your cat to come is when he is hungry. As soon as his dinner is ready to serve, call *"Thomas, come!"* and get his attention, if necessary by clapping your hands or tapping a spoon on the side of his dish. When the cat comes, praise him lavishly, then give him the food. It won't be long before he associates the command with the pleasure of eating.

As soon as your cat comes consistently for meals, command him to come for other reasons. Since his response is patterned for praise and food, try calling him to come to rooms other than the kitchen. When he does come, praise him lavishly and give him a treat. The treat should always be a *small* tidbit that the cat really craves. Give your cat a reason to come at first, and he will show up! Once the cat responds, you need not reward him each time he comes. In fact, rewarding him occasionally often makes him respond more eagerly. If your cat begins to lose interest, however, go back to rewarding him regularly until he comes willingly when called.

## SHOULD CATS WEAR COLLARS?

The advisability of collars for cats has always been under fire on the premise that they snag on tree branches, fences, and other projections and risk choking the animal to death. On the other hand, cats that live indoors often wear collars, complete with attached nameplate or identification tag.

There is a good reason for the collar: the indoor or city cat, however closely guarded, may be stolen or lost if he happens to wriggle out of the house. The identification tag is in a way a status symbol indicating that somebody cares, that somebody grieves when he is gone, that somebody wants him back again. The owner's name and address on his identification tag makes short work of tracing him as has been attested to time and time again by the ASPCA and other shelter custodians.

The homing instinct of animals like cats and dogs has been established as a fact; nevertheless, its degree depends upon the kind of life the animal leads. The cat given his freedom outdoors learns to recognize the landmarks of his neighborhood; thus he comes and goes at will and rarely gets lost. The housebound cat on the other hand has little opportunity to orient himself, and it may be difficult to find his way home without assistance.

## THE RIGHT TYPE OF COLLAR

If a collar is to be worn at all, it should contain an elastic expansion panel to stretch it or be made of Velcro and release quickly under pressure. A collar that expands or releases can prevent a cat from strangling. The free-roaming cat is less apt to suffer snagging if he wears a collar that he can wriggle out of, or one that will free his head and allow him to breathe.

Identification is absolutely essential, especially if your cat goes outdoors. A collar with a metal nameplate, an I.D. tag, or a tube containing a paper with your name, address, and phone number can help identify your cat if he strays from home.

If your cat decides that the collar is absolutely not for him, you might try a lightweight figure-eight or figure "H" harness, about three-eighths of an inch wide, since the directive pull at the shoulders may prove less frightening than at the throat. Do not try to use a dog harness: it will not fit properly. Harnesses are sold according to girth measurement; you must measure around your cat for the correct size.

The much-stroked, much-loved, much-pampered cat has been known to relinquish a modicum of his independent spirit, in which case we may find him willing to submit to the collar or harness and the leash. We can try to trick him into accepting the collar by making a game out of it. Have a favorite toy handy—the simplest of all is a handful of paper crushed into a ball. Throw it around and let the cat pounce on it, or tie a string to it and wig-wag it to attract his attention. Then, if and when he is in a playful mood, put the collar or harness on and get going again with the paper ball. Perhaps in his desire to catch it, he will forget everything else.

Stay close to the cat; do not leave the collar or harness on at first for any length of time. When the ballgame is at its height, remove the collar, praise the cat, then repeat the performance for several days thereafter.

### THE LEASH

You will also need a leash, about three-eighths of an inch wide, made of comfortable material, such as nylon or soft leather. The snap at the end should be a small but sturdy bolt type rather than a clip.

As soon as your cat becomes accustomed to wearing his collar or harness, snap on the leash. Do not attempt to guide the pupil with it. Let him drag it about if he likes, or shake it as if it were a toy. Stay close by to extract him if he gets tangled in something. The next step is to take the leash in your hand and gently guide His Honor as you walk along.

Training any cat to the collar or harness and leash may prove difficult because the very idea of expecting a cat to come and go when and where you direct him is the antithesis of independent feline temperament. Nevertheless, it has been done successfully and has its value. Certain breeds—including Siamese, Colorpoint and Oriental Shorthairs, and Burmese—seem to adapt to leash training more than others.

We cannot expect the leashed cat to walk nonchalantly alongside the highway like a dog. Passersby distract him, and other animals frighten him not only into a desire to run away but perhaps to claw you or the stranger who dares to stroke him. Never drag your cat against his will, and go only as far as he walks comfortably. There are exceptions to the rule, of course, and your cat may be one of them. Try then to walk him in some secluded place. Maybe after awhile he will sense that the leash means that you are nearby for his protection.

Training a cat to do a few tricks is fun for the owner and fun for the cat. On the whole, it is not too difficult *if* the cat is in the mood for learning. The pupil must be at least four or five months old before you begin trick training, so that his mind is sufficiently developed.

Try only simple exercises at first. How far you can progress with more intricate exercises depends upon the temperament and intelligence potential of the pupil as well as upon the skill of the teacher.

Teach one trick at a time. When one lesson has been well learned, always review the first before starting on another. Begin with a trick that the cat already does of his own accord. The lesson here is to induce him to do this trick because you command it. *Roll over* is a case in point.

The average cat likes to be scratched. When you stroke or scratch his stomach, he often rolls over on his back. Kneel on the floor beside the cat. As you stroke him, say quickly and clearly, *"Thomas, roll over!"* and give him a slight push in the direction you want him to roll, then reward him with a treat. Say the phrase again and again, continuing to guide him through the roll with your hands. Repetition instills the command. Each time the pupil obeys, offer him a treat until he learns that rolling over is the move that's being rewarded. Continue each lesson no more than ten minutes.

*Sit up* is another easy trick based upon the strength of the cat's back and hind legs. However, you must start this trick at just the right moment. It is natural for a cat to stand up on his hind legs and reach for a swinging toy with his forelegs. When he keeps at it too long, he tends to sit up rather than stand up; his hind legs tire but his back does not. Thus he does what you want him to do, even before you issue the order. Quickly order him to *Sit up* the instant he appears to tire.

*Waving* is another easy trick, since most cats will naturally swipe at any tidbit that's put near their nose. Hold the treat in your hand, in front of the cat's nose but just out of reach of his front paws. When the cat extends his foreleg to get the treat, move it back and forth several times until he makes a few passes at it, then feed him his reward.

*Shaking hands* is a simple exercise that you can try once your cat has learned to wave. While your cat sits in front of you, extend your hand, palm upward, a few inches from his chest, and say *"Shake hands!"* As soon as he reacts and places his paw in your hand, shake it. Then release the paw, and give him a treat.

Other simple exercises can be taught by the patient and cheerful teacher. Lessons like *Lie down*, *Fetch*, *Jump up on your chair*, and others will serve to develop the pupil's mind as well as give him something interesting to do.

Keep the teaching periods short and regular. A cat has a good memory, but we can hardly expect him to remember his lessons when they are spaced too far apart. Nor can we expect him always to be in a good humor. If, one day, he looks at you with lackluster eyes and, as you issue a command, walks away without looking back, forget the session for twenty-four hours or at least until he has regained his usual cheerful mood.

How can one judge when the cat is in the right frame of mind for lessons to begin? It does not take long to understand the signs of good humor; purring, tail held high, rubbing the body against you, licking your hand lightly, and kneading with the forepaws may all be regarded as signs of happiness or friendly overtures.

## CORRECTING MISBEHAVIOR

Every cat misbehaves occasionally. Just as you praise your cat when he does something proper, so you must discipline him when he does something wrong. When disciplinary action is taken, it must be delivered immediately for the cat to relate the punishment to the crime. As soon as you catch your cat misbehaving, voice your disapproval with a firm "No!" Cats dislike loud noises, and the vocal denunciation should be coupled with a loud clapping of your hands or the smacking of a folded newspaper across your palm. If vocal reprimands alone do not work, they may be accompanied by a few squirts from a spray bottle or water pistol. A vigorous spritz of water is one of the most effective disciplinary measures for cats.

Another way to deal with persistent offenders is to pick up the cat and cradle his body in one arm while holding the scruff of his neck with the other. Shake him once or twice (but never violently) as you voice your disgust with a sharp "No!"

## SOLVING PROBLEMS

The most common undesirable behaviors include chronic clawing on valuable household furnishings, urine spraying, jumping on furniture and kitchen counters, urinating away from the litter box, and raiding trash and garbage cans. Many behavioral problems, by the way, are not caused by misbehavior but by illness. If your cat constantly misbehaves, have him examined by a veterinarian to determine if the condition is caused by pain rather than disobedience.

### CLAWING FURNITURE AND OTHER HOUSEHOLD OBJECTS

The best solution to chronic clawing of furniture, carpeting, and drapes is training the cat to use a scratching post (see page 19). If the cat has not learned to use the post regularly, try anchoring a few inflated balloons to the spot that's being clawed, or drape a sheet of aluminum foil over the area. When your cat reaches up to scratch, the bursting of the balloons or crackling of the foil will frighten him away. When you go out, confine the cat in a room with his post but no furniture to scratch on.

### URINE SPRAYING

Spraying occurs in male cats after sexual maturity. It is a form of territory marking in which a cat backs up to a vertical target, raises and wiggles his tail, then squirts a stream of strong-smelling urine on the object. Inside your house, this unpleasant odor can permeate your furniture, carpets, drapes, and even the walls.

Spraying occurs mainly in unneutered males, but some unspayed females spray also, as do a few altered cats of both sexes. Females spray by crouching down in front and elevating their hind legs.

Neutering will stop the spraying habit in about 85 percent of all cats. If a male cat is neutered before he becomes sexually mature, he is less likely to spray than one that is castrated later in life.

### JUMPING ON FURNITURE OR KITCHEN COUNTERS

Chemical repellents for cats are effective on furniture, but they should not be sprayed on kitchen counters. Try stacking a few baking pans or other noise-making devices on the counter so that they will fall down when your cat jumps up. You can also try anchoring several inflated balloons to the chairs or furniture you don't want your cat to jump on.

### URINATING AWAY FROM THE LITTER BOX

This may be caused by cystitis, diabetes, urinary incontinence in elderly cats, or other illness. *If you have ruled out a possible medical cause*, try feeding your cat at the spot where he is soiling. Let the food dish remain between meals to discourage him from returning to resoil the area. After about a week, resume feeding at the cat's regular place. Should he have a relapse, feed him again at the site of the soiling. It sometimes takes several weeks to solve this problem. In the meantime, keep the litter in the cat's box fresh and clean.

### RAIDING TRASH AND GARBAGE CANS

The odors from trash and garbage cans can be quite tempting to cats. Inflated balloons are the most effective deterrents. Spread some of his favorite food over them, then tape them where he will burst them with his teeth or claws.

# 11
# Practical Home Care

A healthy cat begins as a healthy kitten. When you bring home your new cat, especially if he is a kitten, schedule a visit to the veterinarian for a thorough going-over as soon as possible. The veterinarian can get acquainted with you and your cat and plan an annual health and immunization program. Thereafter, you should take your cat for regular checkups at least once a year—preferably twice annually—because preventive care is the key to good health.

## BE OBSERVANT

Every cat is an individual entity with peculiar characteristics that distinguish him from others. Help your veterinarian by learning the signs of good health. Then, as you get to know your cat, you'll be able to tell if something is not quite right.

### TEN SIGNS OF A HEALTHY CAT

1. GENERAL APPEARANCE: alert, active, lively; good muscle tone.
2. COAT AND SKIN: glossy and unbroken coat, with no bare patches; smooth and supple skin. A healthy cat should groom himself regularly.
3. GAIT: agile and graceful.
4. EYES: clear and bright.
5. NOSE: cool and slightly moist with no secretions.
6. MOUTH: pink gums and lips, not bluish or ashy colored; firmly implanted teeth with no tartar buildup; pleasant smelling breath.
7. EARS: clean and dry, with pale pink skin on the external flaps and inside.
8. BODY: no lumps or masses, especially around the nipples.
9. URINATION: clear yellow, not orange.
10. DEFECATION: stools should be well formed and eliminated regularly.

### WARNING SIGNS

Call your veterinarian if any of the following develop:

1. BEHAVIOR CHANGES: lethargy, lack of normal energy or playfulness; reduced tolerance for exercise; viciousness or irrational behavior; suddenly hiding in closets or other isolated places.
2. CHANGES IN EATING HABITS: excessive weight gain or loss.

3. CHANGES IN WATER INTAKE AND URINATION: unquenchable thirst; changes in urinating habits; constant straining or inability to urinate.

4. CHANGES IN DEFECATION: frequent, bloody, uncontrolled, or forced stools; constipation or inability to defecate.

5. VOMITING: short periods or continual episodes over a long period, especially if vomitus is bloody or accompanied by weakness, pain, or fever.

6. EYE ABNORMALITIES: excessive tearing, cloudy or mucus discharge, film over eyes, sensitivity to light; partial covering of each eye by the nictitating membrane or third eyelid. The nictitating membrane, a small pink flap located at the inner corner of each eye, is usually barely visible. When it becomes enlarged and partially covers the eye, it can be a sign of illness.

7. NOSE: sticky or yellowish discharge.

8. EAR ABNORMALITIES: foul odor, excessive wax, unusual discharge, shaking or tilting of the head, hematoma (a large blister or accumulation of blood beneath the skin) on the ear flap.

9. MOUTH: pale gums or foul breath.

10. PAIN AND LIMPING: pain in getting up or lying down, or when touched or lifted; difficulty in walking.

11. SNEEZING/COUGHING: prolonged sneezing or coughing (other than single episodes).

12. FEVER: temperature over 102.5 degrees Fahrenheit (39 degrees Celsius).

13. LUMPS OR MASSES: swellings or lumps on or beneath the skin, particularly those that are growing rapidly or bleeding; abdominal swelling; tumors of the breasts or testicles.

14. SKIN ABNORMALITIES: hair loss, baldness, open sores, pustules, lesions, excessive external parasite infestation or any other skin problem; intense biting or scratching at the skin and coat.
15. BLEEDING OR DISCHARGES: bleeding from any body part; abnormal discharges from any body opening.
16. CHANGES IN RESPIRATION: difficult or shallow breathing.

When you do take your cat to the veterinarian, be prepared to give an accurate account of the symptoms, the time of the problem's onset, and any other important observations. The more information you can give, the better the veterinarian can diagnose and treat the problem.

### IMMUNIZATION

Kittens and adult cats must be immunized against certain infectious diseases such as feline panleukopenia and highly contagious upper respiratory problems—rhinotracheitis, infection by calici virus, and pneumonitis. If you let your cat roam freely outdoors, vaccination against rabies is recommended, especially if he comes into contact with other free-roaming or wild animals. Cats, dogs, raccoons, skunks, coyotes, foxes, wolves, and bats can be carriers of this deadly disease. Although there has been an increase in the number of rabies cases in certain areas of the country, in many states cats are not required by law to receive this vaccination. Consult your veterinarian about immunization against rabies, even if your cat is housebound.

In 1985, Leukocell®, a vaccine to protect cats

against the feline leukemia virus (see page 122), was introduced after years of work by researchers. It has proven to be safe and effective, and can be given as early as nine weeks of age to any healthy kitten. Your veterinarian can supply more information about this vaccine.

Immunization involves a series of vaccine injections to safeguard a cat's health. *All cats should be vaccinated*, especially those that are housebound, since many highly contagious viruses are airborne and can be carried indoors on people's shoes. The objective of immunization is to trigger the cat's immunity system to produce defensive antibodies. When a vaccine is injected into the cat's body, it causes a mild version of the disease; thereupon tne immune system produces antibodies to fight the virus.

Kittens born to queens that are immune receive fluids from their mother's colostrum (milk produced the first few days after birth), which temporarily helps them produce disease-fighting antibodies until they are weaned. The amount of protection a kitten receives depends on the amount of antibodies his mother has, and this immunity diminishes rapidly. A kitten loses half of it by the time he is two weeks old. Vaccinations pick up where the queen's colostrum leaves off by inducing the kitten to produce his own antibodies.

Most veterinarians like to give a kitten his first vaccinations when he's six to eight weeks old. A second series of inoculations generally takes place at twelve weeks, then a third sequence is given when the kitten reaches sixteen weeks of age. Your veterinarian will decide on a specific schedule for your cat. Vaccination types and schedules vary among veterinarians and are affected by statutes and local conditions.

*Vaccinations are not permanent*. Thereafter, you'll need to take your cat to the veterinarian at least once a year for booster shots.

### FELINE PANLEUKOPENIA (FPL)

Feline panleukopenia (FPL), also called infectious enteritis and feline distemper, is a highly contagious and potentially fatal viral disease.

The virus is passed from cat to cat by direct or indirect contact. Infection can occur when direct contact is made with the blood, urine, fecal material, nasal secretions, vomitus, and even the fleas of infected animals. The virus can also be concealed in an infected animal's bedding, feeding dishes, cages, and other objects, as well as on the clothing and shoes of his handlers. Pet shops, catteries, humane shelters, and other places where cats are gathered together in groups seem to be the main sources of infection of FPL today.

Unvaccinated cats of all ages are susceptible to feline panleukopenia, although the disease is most common in young kittens. Symptoms appear within two to ten days after exposure and include a high fever accompanied by depression, loss of appetite, frothy vomiting, and dehydration. An infected cat often appears to be hanging over his water dish due to extreme thirst, and he often cries from abdominal pain. As the disease progresses, other signs may include anemia and bloody diarrhea.

The prognosis for young kittens is poor. The death rate for those under sixteen weeks of age is about 75 percent. Older cats have a better chance of survival if treatment is begun early. Treatment consists of intensive fluid therapy for the dehydration and antibiotics to control secondary bacterial infections.

### UPPER RESPIRATORY DISEASES

Feline upper respiratory diseases are also highly contagious. Like panleukopenia, pet shops, boarding catteries and kennels, humane shelters, and other places where cats are quartered in groups seem to be the main sources of infection.

Upper respiratory diseases are caused by a number of organisms that are spread through the air or by direct or indirect contact. The clinical signs vary depending on which organism is responsible. Most of the problems are caused by two agents: the feline viral rhinotracheitis (FVR) virus and feline calici virus (FVC). Basically, the symptoms are the same—sneezing, runny eyes and nose, coughing, loss of appetite, lethargy, and depression—so it is difficult to distinguish between them. These diseases have an extremely high mortality rate in young kittens. Safe and effective vaccines are available for the following three upper respiratory diseases:

*Feline viral rhinotracheitis* (FVR) is the most common and serious of the upper respiratory diseases. It attacks the nasal chambers, the conjunctiva, and the trachea. Symptoms appear within two to ten days after exposure and include intense sneezing, eye and nose discharges that are liquid at first and later become thick and purulent, swelling of the eyelids, and a harsh cough. Excessive salivation is also seen, and there is a fever of over 104 degrees Fahrenheit (40 degrees Celsius) in many cases, accompanied by depression and loss of appetite. Sometimes a cat will develop painful ulcers inside the mouth that make eating difficult.

Treatment involves keeping the eyes and nose clear, intravenous fluid therapy, antibiotics to fight secondary infection, and certain special medications to make the cat more comfortable. Cats that recover from rhinotracheitis may suffer from frequent minor cold symptoms.

There are many strains of *feline calici virus* (FCV) and these vary in their harmfulness. Some can produce pneumonia and a disease as severe as FVR, while others cause only mild infections. Symptoms appear from one to nine days after exposure and are similar to those of FVR, including ulcers on the tongue and inside the mouth that interfere with eating and cause the cat to lose weight. Treatment includes antibiotics to combat secondary infection, and fluid and nutritional therapy.

*Feline pneumonitis* (FPN), another infectious upper respiratory disease, is caused by *Chlamydia psittaci,* a rickettsial organism that is something between a virus and a bacterium. It is less common than FVR or FCV. Symptoms appear from six to fifteen days after exposure and resemble those of a cold in human beings: red, bloodshot eyes, sniffling, sneezing, swelling of the eyelids, discharge from the eyes and nose, and fever. The cat will have difficulty in breathing and may make rasping sounds with each breath.

Treatment includes antibiotic and fluid therapy, and other medications to make the cat more comfortable.

### RABIES

Rabies seldom results in human fatalities in the United States today, but it remains a potentially serious public health problem. More than 20,000 Americans have to undergo rabies treatments each year as a result of exposure to potentially rabid animals. During the last few years, the number of reported cases of rabies in cats has surpassed that in dogs.

Rabies is caused by a virus. It is spread through the saliva of an infected animal and in no other way. All warm-blooded animals can spread rabies. Rabid animals infect other animals by biting them. This means that your cat will only get rabies *if he is actually bitten by a rabid animal or infected by the animal's saliva through an open wound*. Rabies can also be transmitted from animals to man by a bite from a rabid animal. The wound is contaminated with the virus found in the saliva of the infected animal. The incubation period varies from ten days to several months, depending on the location of the bite and how long the virus takes to reach the brain.

Although there are two forms of rabies, furious and dumb, most cats experience the furious form. The first symptom is usually a marked change in the cat's personality and behavior. He may become restless and search for a hiding place in a dark corner. For the next several days he becomes vicious and eagerly attacks anything in his path including people and other animals. Loud noises or bright lights may induce biting seizures.

If the disease progresses to the paralytic state, the cat's throat muscles become so paralyzed that he cannot swallow, and he salivates profusely. It is during this period that he appears to be frothing at the mouth. Finally, the body and legs become progressively immobilized. There is a lack of coordination, then collapse, coma, and death.

If your cat should show any of these symptoms, or if you know he has been bitten by a free-roaming or wild animal, you must handle him with all possible care. Throw a blanket over him (to keep him from biting you), gather him up, and shut him in his cage or a room. Then call your veterinarian at once. If you are bitten, consult your physician *immediately* and follow his advice.

There is no cure, and rabies is always fatal when it

appears in an animal. It can be prevented, however, by vaccination and periodic reimmunization.

### FELINE LEUKEMIA VIRUS (FeLV)

Feline leukemia virus, known as FeLV, is the most deadly infectious disease of domestic cats today. It is transmitted from cat to cat primarily through the saliva, urine, feces, and respiratory secretions. Prolonged close contact is necessary to spread the virus from an infected to an uninfected cat. The sharing of water dishes, food bowls, and litter boxes, plus licking and biting, are probably the major sources of transmission and infection. The virus can also cross through the placenta from a queen to her unborn kittens; it can also be passed in her milk after the kittens are born.

Once the virus infects a healthy cat, it gravitates to the bone marrow, where it lives and grows in the cells. In many cases, it suppresses the cat's immune system and predisposes him to a host of infections and secondary problems in much the same way that AIDS affects humans.

The most common signs of feline leukemia are loss of appetite, weight loss, persistent gum infection, pale mucous membranes, anemia, persistent fever, weakness, lethargy, and difficulty in breathing. A veterinarian can make a fast and reliable diagnosis by testing a sample of the cat's blood. Some infected cats can carry the virus for life yet show no signs of illness themselves. These are a continuing risk for catteries and multiple-cat households because they can spread the virus, too. For this reason, cats that come in contact with other cats should be routinely tested to be sure they are FeLV negative.

After many years of research by Dr. Richard Olsen

and his staff at Ohio State University in cooperation with Norden Laboratories, Leukocell®, a feline leukemia virus vaccine, was released in 1985. This broad-spectrum vaccine protects cats against FeLV, as well as the FeLV-associated diseases, such as infectious peritonitis, respiratory disease, FeLV panleukopenialike syndrome, reproductive failure, thymic atrophy (fading kitten syndrome), and lymphoid tumor development.

Three intramuscular injections are usually given: the first at nine weeks of age or older, the second three weeks later, and the third after three months. An annual booster is recommended to maintain immunity. Cats should be tested before vaccination, for the new vaccine will not benefit cats that are already infected with feline leukemia virus.

### FELINE INFECTIOUS PERITONITIS (FIP)

Feline infectious peritonitis is another disease that has a high mortality rate in infected cats. It is caused by a virus and spread by direct contact or through the air. There are two forms of the disease—wet and dry. The onset of FIP is gradual and marked by discharges from the eyes and nose, loss of appetite, weight loss, fever, depression, and weakness. In the wet form, the abdomen and chest become inflamed and painful due to fluid buildup. There is no fluid accumulation in the dry form; this form is reflected through inflammatory lesions in the eyes, brain, kidneys and liver, and paralysis.

The virus causes an immune system reaction. Cats under three are most often affected, and mysteriously, about 40 percent of all cats with FIP are also infected with feline leukemia virus, which may harm their ability to ward off FIP. Treatment consists of fluid, antibiotic, and nutritional therapy. An occasional cat may recover, but treatment seldom is successful and FIP is usually fatal. Efforts to produce a vaccine for this disease so far have not been successful.

### FELINE INFECTIOUS ANEMIA (FIA)

Feline infectious anemia is a disease that strikes cats of all ages but most often young males between one and three years old. FIA is spread by a small protozoan parasite, *Hemobartonella felis*, which infects and destroys the cat's red blood cells. Although the method of transmission is not totally understood, evidence indicates that it can be transferred from the blood of a pregnant queen to her kittens inside the womb. The microscopic parasite can also be spread by fleas, mosquitoes, and other blood-sucking insects, or by cat bites.

The onset of FIA is gradual: The most common signs are loss of appetite, excessive thirst, listlessness, and weakness. The blood-cell loss is manifested by anemia, and the cat develops a high fever and becomes weak and emaciated.

Diagnosis is made by testing the cat's blood for the presence of the parasite. If FIA is discovered early, the recovery rate is good. Treatment involves giving antibiotics and vitamins. Blood transfusions and intravenous fluid therapy will be necessary for severely anemic cats; however, these seldom survive.

### FELINE UROLOGIC SYNDROME (FUS)

Feline urologic syndrome, or FUS, is a complex urinary tract problem that affects cats of all ages and all breeds. Acute or chronic bladder inflammation and infection (cystitis), urethral obstruction, and kidney disease are all part of the FUS complex. These are said to account for from 5 to 10 percent of all veterinary hospital admissions.

The signs of feline urologic syndrome include

1. Changes in urinary habits, such as forgetting to use the litter box or soiling in unusual places.
2. Frequent and hard straining to pass urine, or the passing of small quantities of urine. The cat will squat in a hunched-up position very close to the ground or his litter box in an effort to urinate.
3. Distraught behavior and cries of pain.
4. Urine that is blood-stained or that has a strong, ammonialike odor.
5. Excessive licking of the penis or vulva.

When urine passes from the body, it flows from the bladder through a tube known as the urethra. In females, the urine empties into the vulva; in males, it streams through the penis. When urine is retained too long, its normally acid pH changes to alkaline. Salts (especially from food with high levels of ash and magnesium) form struvite crystals that turn into gritty substances known as stones or plugs. These block the urethral passage and stop the flow of urine.

Urethral obstruction is more common in males than in females, because their urethras are long and narrow. Signs that the urethra is blocked and that the condition is severe are vomiting, depression, dehydration, urinelike odor to the breath, and a painful and distended bladder. *This is an emergency; go immediately to a veterinarian,* for a cat may die if he cannot empty his bladder.

It is not clear what actually causes FUS, and many factors may be involved—including excessive mineral intake, too much dry food, alkaline urine, viral and bacterial urinary tract infections, anatomic defects, slight fluid consumption, urine retention, obesity, stress, and castration of the male cat.

FUS can be treated successfully when it is detected early. Treatment of cats with this obstruction involves a combination of antibiotics to treat bacterial infections, urinary acidifiers, foods low in ash and magnesium, increased water consumption, and minimizing stress. Those with urinary obstructions require urethral catheterization, intravenous fluids, and medications.

### INTERNAL PARASITES

There are several kinds of worms and protozoa (single-celled organisms) that can infect cats: roundworms, hookworms, threadworms, lungworms, *coccidia*, *giardia*, and *toxoplasma gondii*. It is wise to know something about the different types of internal parasites and how they affect a cat's health.

### ROUNDWORMS

Roundworms are the most common internal parasites of cats. Two kinds infect cats: *Toxocara cati*, which affects cats only, and *Toxascaris leonina*, which affects cats and dogs. Roundworms are white worms, two to six inches long, that are easy to see in the stool or vomitus.

The life cycle of the roundworm is complex. Cats can become infected after ingesting roundworm eggs from contaminated soil. Following ingestion, the eggs hatch in the upper small intestine, penetrate the intestinal wall, and enter the bloodstream where they reach the right chambers of the heart. Then they migrate to the pulmonary arteries and into the lungs. They continue to grow as they ascend the respiratory tract and are coughed up and reswallowed, returning to the small intestine to complete their maturity. Once mature, adult females can lay several thousand eggs per day that pass in the cat's stool.

In female cats, some of the *Toxocara cati* larvae (but not *Toxascaris leonina*) are not coughed up and do not develop into adults but remain dormant in the body tissues. During pregnancy, some of the dormant larvae become active and may cross the placenta and enter the fetuses. After birth, the larvae migrate to the kitten's intestines and mature. Larvae can also be transmitted to nursing kittens via their mother's milk. If the kittens are infested before birth or while nursing, they can pass roundworm eggs at three weeks of age.

Roundworm infestation is especially debilitating to kittens. Symptoms include overall weakness, malnutrition, and dull coat. The kittens may be ravenous but remain thin and develop potbellied or distended abdomens. Infected kittens have respiratory difficulties and discharges from the eyes. They may cough and vomit a few roundworms, or have diarrhea and pass them out in the stool.

Roundworms have public health significance, since the larvae can cause *visceral larva migrans* in humans, especially children. Infestation occurs when ingested eggs hatch in the intestines, penetrate the intestinal wall, and reach the bloodstream. They migrate through the body, causing considerable damage that can be debilitating. If the larvae migrate into the eye, they can cause permanent damage. Infection often occurs when children and infected pets live and play in the same areas. Children's sandboxes should be covered to prevent contamination by infected cats.

### HOOKWORMS

Hookworms are small parasites that live in the cat's intestines where they "hook" onto the intestinal wall and suck the blood. Although hookworms are less common in cats than in dogs, a heavy infestation can lead to anemia and even death. Cats can become infested in two ways: by eating soil or feces contaminated with infective larvae, or through skin penetration. The latter sometimes causes a reaction that develops into a moist dermatitis. Hookworms can be present in newborn kittens that have been infected in the womb from their mother. Symptoms of infection include emaciation, pale gums (due to anemia), vomiting, and intermittent bloody diarrhea.

### TAPEWORMS

Tapeworms live in a cat's intestines where they attach their heads to the intestinal wall. Unlike roundworms and hookworms, tapeworms require an intermediate host to develop their growth and larval stages. The most common hosts are the fleas that live in the cat's fur. In the process of self-grooming, the cat licks his fur and swallows fleas.

Although tapeworms are virtually impossible to detect by microscopic examination, they can often be seen with the naked eye as flat, creamy-colored segments when they leave the rectum. Then they become dry and brownish, and look like grains of rice in the hair. You might find a few sticking around the cat's rectum, or to his bed.

Tapeworms may become several feet long and continue to grow unless the head part is eliminated. Symptoms vary with severity of infection, age, and physical condition of the cat, and include a dull and brittle coat, listlessness, emaciation, and diarrhea. Infection also causes itching and irritation at the rectum, and the cat will often bite himself to gain relief.

### OTHER WORMS

Other internal parasites that are occasionally seen in cats are threadworms and lungworms. It is believed that threadworms *(Strongyloides)* can be transmitted through the milk of an infected queen. Cats become infected with lungworms by eating snails or slugs—the intermediate hosts of these parasites. Lungworms live in a cat's lungs and cause chronic respiratory disease. The cat coughs, has difficulty breathing, loses his appetite, and becomes emaciated.

### *COCCIDIA* AND *GIARDIA*

*Coccidia* and *giardia* are both protozoan parasites (one-celled organisms) that live in the intestinal tract. Both cause diarrhea. *Coccidia* most often infest young kittens while *giardia* infect both kittens and adults. Both organisms multiply rapidly in the intestines and are transferred from cat to cat via the stool. Young infected kittens quickly become weak and emaciated.

### TREATMENT FOR WORMS
### AND PROTOZOAN PARASITES

Your veterinarian can determine by microscopic examination of a fresh stool sample if your cat has roundworms, hookworms, or protozoan parasites. Tapeworms are tough to detect in this manner, but you can often tell when your cat is infected because segments break off and pass out in the bowel movements.

Once the type of internal parasite is identified, the veterinarian will dispense the correct anthelmintic. There are special medicines for each kind of intestinal parasite, but the specific type must be identified before the right drug can be prescribed. Worm medicine is powerful stuff, irritating to the stomach and intestines, weakening to the patient, and often dangerous unless given in the proper amount—carefully measured by the age, size, strength, and condition of the individual cat.

It is safer to let your veterinarian worm your cat for you and not advisable to try "over-the-counter" remedies. Be sure you follow your veterinarian's instructions to the letter. If he says your cat should not eat for a certain number of hours before giving the medicine, make sure the cat fasts, with no tidbits or even milk to "tide him over."

### TOXOPLASMOSIS

Toxoplasmosis, caused by the protozoan parasite *Toxoplasma gondii*, is a potentially serious disease. Although it affects many animals, only cats spread toxoplasmosis via infective oocytes or egg spores shed in their feces. The parasite lives in an infected cat's intestines and produces a variety of symptoms including diarrhea, poor appetite, fever, and enlarged lymph nodes. Many infected cats, however, display no signs of toxoplasmosis but can still pass it on to other animals and (under certain conditions) to humans. The disease can also be spread by handling or eating raw meat. Cooking the meat kills the protozoa.

Toxoplasmosis is most dangerous to women in their first trimester of pregnancy as it may cause miscarriage or congenital malformation in the fetus. Pregnant women should avoid emptying or cleaning the litter box and should wash their hands thoroughly after touching the cat or his belongings.

The cat's fecal matter should be scooped out of the litter box and disposed of immediately. It takes forty-eight hours for the oocytes to become infective after a bowel movement by an infected cat. In the oocyte stage, the organism can also survive in soil. In areas where there are many outdoor cats, wear gloves while gardening or cleaning sandboxes to avoid touching contaminated soil.

The best way to protect your cat from becoming infected with toxoplasma organisms is to feed only commercially prepared cat foods. Don't let the cat eat raw meat or kill birds or rodents since they could be diseased. A blood test is available to determine if the cat is carrying the organism.

### HEARTWORM DISEASE

Heartworms are harmful internal parasites that live in the right ventricle and pulmonary artery of the cat's heart. It was once believed that heartworms infected only dogs, but now it is known that cats are also susceptible to the same species that infects dogs as well as foxes, coyotes, and other animals.

Heartworm is transmitted by the bite of a mosquito (about sixty species are capable of carrying the disease). The cycle works something like this: When a mosquito feeds on an infected animal, it ingests blood that contains an immature heartworm form called *microfilariae*. These incubate inside the mosquito and, in as little as two weeks, become infective larvae. The mosquito bites a cat and passes the infective larvae into the cat's bloodstream. The larvae migrate through the cat's body tissues and enter the heart where they mature and reproduce *microfilariae* that enter the bloodstream and begin the life cycle again.

Signs of heartworm disease include frequent coughing, listlessness, fatigue, labored breathing, and emaciation. Most symptoms are generally not apparent, however, until the disease has reached a serious stage. By this time the damage to the cat's vital organs may be so severe that he cannot be saved. Therefore, early diagnosis is important.

To determine if your cat has heartworm, have your veterinarian examine a sample of his blood to see if any *microfilariae* are present. A cat may occasionally have adult heartworms but no *microfilariae*. In this case, X-ray and other tests will be necessary to confirm infection.

Treatment of heartworm disease in cats is quite serious: The mortality rate is much higher than that in dogs. Prevention is the only solution to the problem. If you live in an area heavily infested with mosquitoes and your cat goes outside, consult your veterinarian about preventive measures.

### FIRST AID KIT

A first aid kit can help save your cat's life in an emergency. The following items should be kept at home, in a clearly labeled box or carton, in a location known to every family member. Replace them when they are used. Take them with you when you travel with your cat:

- STERILE GAUZE DRESSINGS: generally in sizes 3 by 3 inches and 4 by 4 inches to protect wounds and help stop bleeding.
- GAUZE BANDAGE: 1- or 2-inch-wide rolls.
- FIRST AID TAPE: to hold dressings and bandages in place.
- SELF-ADHESIVE BANDAGE: to hold dressings in place.
- COTTON/COTTON BALLS/COTTON SWABS: for applying ointments or swabbing wounds.
- 3% HYDROGEN PEROXIDE: to clean minor wounds and to induce vomiting.
- FIRST AID CREAM OR ANTIBACTERIAL SKIN OINTMENT: to soothe minor rashes and burns.
- SOAP OR PHISODERM: for cleaning wounds.
- ACTIVATED CHARCOAL: to absorb poisons.
- KAOPECTATE: to control diarrhea.
- PEPTO-BISMOL OR MAALOX: to relieve vomiting or upset stomach.
- MINERAL OIL: to clean your cat's ears.
- HAIRBALL REMEDY.
- CHILDREN'S MEDICINE SPOON OR SYRINGE (with needle removed) for administering liquids.
- RECTAL THERMOMETER: petroleum jelly is a good lubricant for the thermometer.
- TWEEZERS: to remove foreign objects and ticks from your cat's skin.
- NEEDLE-NOSE PLIERS: to remove partially swallowed objects that are caught in the throat.
- BLUNT-TIPPED SCISSORS.

### EMERGENCIES

The following are some of the problems and emergencies that cat owners may have to contend with.

## VOMITING

Vomiting occurs occasionally in cats of all ages because they can vomit at will. Many times the cat simply wants to regurgitate something because he dislikes it.

Persistent vomiting, however, can be a symptom of many cat diseases, among them kidney and liver problems, intestinal inflammations, digestive upsets, feline panleukopenia, and feline infectious enteritis. Too much food is a common cause: the cure, less food fed at more frequent intervals. Worms can also be responsible; getting rid of them solves the problem. Then there are what may be called mechanical causes, among them poisoning and drug intoxication (see page 138).

To treat vomiting, withhold food and almost all water for twelve to twenty-four hours to rest the stomach. After awhile, let the cat lick a few ice cubes if he is thirsty. During the fast, an antacid product with a protective coating action—such as Pepto-Bismol or Maalox—given according to your veterinarian's direction, will help soothe stomach irritation.

If the vomiting stops after twenty-four hours, give small amounts of bland food such as lean chopped beef or chicken that has been boiled to remove the fat, rice, or strained baby foods.

Do not experiment with the persistent vomiter too long, however. Better see your veterinarian if it doesn't clear up within twenty-four hours. And if blood is vomited, especially a profuse amount, or if blood clots are present in the vomitus, seek veterinary assistance immediately.

### DIARRHEA

Diarrhea often results from a number of systemic and other problems. If it happens only once or twice, it may be nothing more than a slight intestinal upset. A sudden change in diet can bring it on; a switch from one brand of food to another is best done over a period of several days, where the new food is gradually mixed in increasing amounts with the old. Diarrhea often results from nervousness or fright brought on by unaccustomed journeys or excitement. Partially decomposed food and food allergies will cause it, too.

Continuing diarrhea can be an indication of feline panleukopenia or feline infectious enteritis; intestinal parasites are also a major cause. Serious diarrhea involving several daily evacuations and/or evil-smelling or blood-streaked stools should be treated immediately by a veterinarian.

Mild or occasional cases may be relieved by the same treatment as for vomiting: withholding food for twelve to twenty-four hours and allowing the cat to drink only small quantities of water. Kaopectate, given according to your veterinarian's instructions, will help to settle the stomach and the irritated linings of the intestines, and stop the diarrhea. Feed small quantities of bland food after twelve hours. If the diarrhea has not stopped after twenty-four hours, call your veterinarian.

### CONSTIPATION

Although constipation is more common in elderly cats and meticulous longhaired self-groomers, it can appear in cats of all ages. Constipation develops when solid waste products accumulate in the cat's intestines and cannot be evacuated easily. The cat strains hard to pass the mass and often cries out in pain.

One common cause of constipation, especially in longhairs, is a hairball in the intestines (see page 36). Other causes include poor diet, lack of exercise, intestinal obstructions other than a hairball, loss of muscle tone in old cats, and other illness.

When constipation occurs, one teaspoon of Milk of Magnesia for an average-sized cat should help to clear the intestines. If the cat is still constipated after a day or so, call your veterinarian. Do not experiment with other human laxatives; some contain ingredients that can be harmful to cats.

Roughage (in the form of leafy vegetables) and bulkier foods will help to stimulate the colon and add form to the stools. If your cat suffers from chronic constipation, the veterinarian may recommend using a stool softener once in awhile. But do not give one to your cat unless told to do so by your veterinarian.

## BURNS AND SCALDS

Most animal burns and scalds result from contact with direct heat—hot water, grease, or other liquids—and chemical agents, or from chewing wires. A burn is caused by dry heat, such as flame, while a scald is caused by moist heat—having hot liquids spilled on the body, for instance. Emergency treatment includes the following:

*Thermal*—For heat burns, help cool the area by applying cold water or an ice pack for twenty to thirty minutes. Apply an antibacterial ointment. Do not apply butter, margarine, grease, salad oil, or other home remedies; these will trap the heat and delay healing.

*Chemical*—For burns from corrosive chemicals, *flush the skin with quantities of cool water*. If the substance contained an alkali, follow with a rinse of equal parts vinegar and water. If the substance contained an acid, follow with a baking soda rinse (two to three tablespoons per quart of warm water). Do not use any solvents on the skin.

*Electrical*—Disconnect the wire from its power source if it is touching the cat's body. If you can't unplug the cord or locate the fuse box, wrap a heavy towel around your hand or use a ruler, broom handle, or other nonconductor of electricity to push the wire out of the mouth or away from the body. Keep the cat warm and get veterinary attention at once.

Extensive external burns from fire and scalding liquids can be a serious emergency. Keep the cat warm and quiet and get immediate veterinary treatment.

### COUGH

A cough is serious, whether or not breathing is difficult. It can be a sign of several different illnesses and diseases, including bronchitis and viral respiratory disease, roundworm infestation, allergic reaction, obstruction in the throat, and heart disease (especially in old cats). A cough may be no more than a barely audible hack, or it may be accompanied by fever, labored breathing, and nasal or eye discharges. Consult your veterinarian immediately. Do not administer human cough suppressant medicines.

### POISONING

We frequently think of poison as a dose planted by a fiend to kill the cat or dog next door. Such cases are rare. More often someone's ignorance or carelessness causes a cat to poison himself. The garbage can, too, so attractive to all cats, must bear its share of blame for such tragedies. And occasionally, a cat comes to grief when, with the best of intentions, he is doctored with remedies from the family medicine chest. Never give your cat "people" medicine without first checking with your veterinarian.

Poisoning can affect a cat suddenly when large doses are swallowed, or it can sicken him gradually if taken in small amounts. While ingestion of different toxins produces various symptoms, some of the most visible signs of poisoning include trembling, excessive thirst, increased salivation, dilated pupils, frequent swallowing, mouth odor, vomiting, staggering gait, panting, diarrhea, paralysis, convulsions, and coma.

The most common household danger for cats is poisoning. They can become poisoned by chewing, tasting, or swallowing toxic substances out of curiosity or boredom, or when they are teething or hungry. Every room in the house, including the garage, contains items that are potentially dangerous to pets. Prevent accidental poisoning by keeping cleaning agents, pesticides, chemicals, and other dangerous substances out of your cat's reach.

For instance, ethylene glycol—the active ingredient in antifreeze, Sterno, and windshield deicers—is one of the most deadly substances for cats. They are attracted to its sweet, syrupy taste. Symptoms of ingestion include vomiting, mental confusion, progressive depression, and eventual collapse. If treatment is not started early, the cat will usually experience kidney failure and die. When products containing ethylene glycol are stored in the garage, they should be tightly sealed and placed out of your cat's reach.

Today, because of a general interest in gardening and houseplants, cats come into contact with many plant varieties. Most of them are harmless, but there are over seven hundred types of plants in this hemisphere that can be potentially toxic (even deadly) to cats. Because many cats nibble on house or garden plants, it is sensible to learn which ones can be dangerous.

### FIRST AID FOR SWALLOWED POISONS

First aid depends on the kind of poison ingested. When a noncaustic substance is ingested, an emetic is given like any liquid medicine (see page 156) to make the cat vomit. Giving hydrogen peroxide is an efficient and safe way to make a cat vomit in an emergency situation. If the cat is conscious, give him one-half to one teaspoon every five minutes until vomiting occurs. A strong solution of table salt mixed in water is another good emetic although not as effective as hydrogen peroxide.

If the cat has swallowed corrosive acid or alkali, gasoline, kerosene, drain cleaner, paint thinner, other petroleum distillates, or strychnine, do not attempt to make him throw up. Instead, dilute the poison by giving him milk, whipped egg whites, Milk of Magnesia, or water to help delay further absorption.

The veterinarian within easy reach is a godsend, for there is no time to be lost. Act with all speed if your cat is to be saved. If you know the particular kind of poison your cat has eaten, take along the package. This will help the veterinarian choose the right antidote. Packages con-

taining poisonous materials clearly state the correct anti-
dotes on the labels.

If you cannot reach your veterinarian immediately,
give the antidote listed on the package label, or call your
local Poison Control Center to learn the correct emergency treatment. You should be able to find the Poison
Control Center number for your area listed on the inside
front cover of the telephone directory. If you do not know
what the cat swallowed, dilute the poison by giving two
teaspoons of activated charcoal mixed with water or
milk, then go the nearest veterinarian as quickly as possible.

### ENCOUNTERS WITH SKUNKS

If your cat has had an argument with a skunk, you
will want to take immediate steps to get rid of the odor,
for your own sake as well as the cat's. Skunk spray can be
very irritating, and you may see your cat pawing his eyes
in misery. In such a case, flush the eyes with lukewarm
water or eyewash solution, then put a little ophthalmic
ointment into each eye. Then shampoo the cat as thoroughly as possible, rinse thoroughly, and towel the excess
moisture from his coat. To remove the skunk odor, mix
about five to six ounces of Massengill douche powder or
liquid (available at most pharmacies) in a gallon of warm
water. Pour the mixture slowly and thoroughly over the
cat, taking care that it doesn't run into his eyes. Don't
rinse it off; let it dry on the hair. Two or three treatments
may be necessary.

## PORCUPINE QUILLS

The cat that tangles with a porcupine is going to be stuck with quills, particularly around the head and face. The quills are barbed and will become more deeply embedded if they are not removed promptly. This is painful for the cat, and he must be properly restrained.

When just a few quills are present, you can remove them yourself by grasping each quill close to the skin with needle-nose pliers and twisting it out carefully with a steady pull. Pull straight backward, not at an angle, or the quill will break apart. Work slowly and be sure to remove the entire quill, then flush the wound with hydrogen peroxide.

Check inside the mouth carefully; usually these and any deeply embedded quills will have to be removed by a veterinarian while the cat is anesthetized.

### INSECT STINGS

Stings by bees, wasps, and hornets are common. Those on the body are not so serious since the coat serves as protection, but those on the head, where the hair is often sparser, can cause pain and swelling.

Extract the stinger with tweezers if you can see it. Then apply a thin pastelike mixture of baking soda and water, or boric acid powder and water, to help relieve itching. Cold compresses will help to reduce swelling, which may not go down for twenty-four hours.

## SEIZURES OR "FITS"

Seizures, or involuntary paroxysmal disturbances of brain function characterized by violent spasms or contractions of muscles, occasionally occur in cats. They may result from a variety of causes, including hereditary predisposition, epilepsy, encephalitis, hypoglycemia, hypocalcemia, brain tumor, and exposure to certain drugs and poisons.

An attack may last for only a few moments as the cat becomes restless, shakes, stiffens, stares glassy eyed, and froths at the mouth. Or he may stagger and roll over on his side as his legs continue to contract, lose control of his bladder or bowels, and become unconscious. Remove the sufferer to a quiet, semidark room, or place him in a crate where he cannot injure himself. After the seizure, a cat can exhibit a number of behavioral changes, including confusion, depression, and fatigue.

Repeated or prolonged seizures should be considered a serious emergency that requires immediate veterinary attention. Whether the seizure is mild or severe, however, it should be followed by a complete physical checkup and perhaps a neurological evaluation.

## CHOKING OR SWALLOWING FOREIGN OBJECTS

It is not unusual for kittens to eat things they shouldn't—the removable parts of toys, for instance, bones, stones, and other small things—that can become lodged in the esophagus or swallowed. If you can get to the veterinarian immediately, so much the better. He can look inside with an endoscope and see exactly what has been swallowed and where it is lodged. Surgery may be necessary.

If help is not available and the object is lodged deep in the throat, open the mouth and try to retrieve it with your fingers or needle-nose pliers. If you cannot, try the Heimlich Maneuver: Lay the cat on his side, then place the palms of your hands on each side of his abdomen just *below* the rib cage. Press into the abdomen with a sharp upward thrust to expel the object. Repeat if necessary. Check inside the mouth for the object and remove it if you can.

### HEATSTROKE

Heatstroke occurs when a cat retains too much heat in his body. It is frequently caused by confining a cat in a hot area without adequate ventilation.

Prompt action is necessary to reduce your cat's temperature to normal. Excessively high temperatures can be tolerated for only a short time before severe central nervous system, heart, and brain damage will result. Cool the body by immersing the cat (excluding the head, of course) in a cool water bath, then get veterinary help as soon as possible. Assemble a couple of ice packs and have someone hold them on the back of the cat's neck and on his abdomen while you drive him to the veterinarian.

### WOUNDS AND BLEEDING

There are two types of wounds: closed and open. A closed wound is an injury in which there is no break in the skin. The tissues beneath the skin may have been injured by a blow from a blunt object, an automobile accident, or a fall from a high place. The danger of infection is not great since closed wounds are subject to little contamination. A closed wound may be a minor injury—a bruise, for example—that may damage the soft tissues beneath the skin, or it may be serious and cause internal bleeding and extensive damage to deeper tissues and organs.

Open wounds are those that involve breaks in the cat's skin. They can range from slight abrasions or scrapes, in which the surface of the skin is lightly scratched—possibly causing superficial bleeding—to deep lacerations and punctures, where there is a danger of massive bleeding that must be controlled or stopped to prevent death.

Lacerations and wounds on the skin surface usually result in minimal bleeding. Wash the wound with soap and water. If the injury is a puncture, flush out the area with hydrogen peroxide to remove bacteria or other foreign matter. Carefully clip the hair around the wound with blunt-tipped scissors. Bandage the wound with gauze and tape to keep it from becoming contaminated. Clean, flush, and redress the wound every day. Check carefully for the presence of infection. Call your veterinarian promptly if the wound does become infected.

Deep wounds that cause profuse bleeding or hemorrhaging from any part of the body should be considered an emergency. If an artery has been severed, bright red blood will spurt from the wound in time with the heartbeat. Blood escaping from a vein will be much darker in color and will ooze. Use a pressure bandage: place a clean cloth or sterile gauze bandage over the wound and apply manual pressure until the bleeding stops, then seek veterinary help immediately. The wound probably will require stitches.

### ANIMAL BITES

Cats are often bitten by other cats or dogs. The severity of the bite depends on the location of the wound, whether it is a puncture or a tear, and the size of the animal that did the biting.

Animal bites can be painful and potentially dangerous if the wound is a deep puncture. When an animal's tooth penetrates the cat's skin, it can cause external tissue damage and also internal damage to muscles and blood vessels that may not be readily apparent. Bites from other cats can be serious, too. Cats have a great deal of bacteria in their mouths, and their bites are likely to cause severe infections. They may look like insignificant punctures and heal quickly on the skin surface, but, because the wound is unable to drain, an abscess can form underneath. Abscesses can go inward or outward, and when they extend to deeper tissue, the infection can enter the bloodstream and cause septicemia. Any bite wound should be cleaned immediately and thoroughly with hot water and soap, then flushed with hydrogen peroxide to remove bacteria or other foreign matter. Large wounds will usually require sutures; take the cat to the veterinarian as soon as possible.

# 12

# Nursing and Special Care

The average cat is a remarkably sturdy animal. Yet there are occasions when he does fall ill and needs careful and patient nursing to bring him back to health.

The healthy cat runs and plays, is bright and reasonably fearless. His face is expressive, his eyes bright and clear, his nostrils cool and slightly moist. The insides of his ears are pale pink; a little wax is normal, but excessive amounts are not. His breath should smell pleasant, and the tissues inside his mouth should also be pink. His skin is smooth and supple, and his coat is glossy. He eats eagerly and drinks rather sparingly. There is a certain springiness about him that shows pleasure in all he does.

It's not always possible to detect incipient illness, for a cat does not go around complaining. He may suddenly stop his mischievous ways and appear listless or out of sorts. Instead of showing the usual interest in his toys, he may seek out dark corners as if he were trying to hide. On the other hand, obvious signs of illness, such as sticky eyes, runny nose, coughing, vomiting, and diarrhea may be evident.

You can help your veterinarian by learning the signs of good health. Every cat is a distinct being with particular characteristics that distinguish him from others. Once you learn what is normal for your cat, the subtle changes in general appearance, behavior, temperature, and respiration that precede illness will be readily apparent.

A cat's stools, for instance, should be brown in color and well formed. A kitten may defecate three to four times a day, an adult cat once; don't worry as long as color and consistency are right. If the stools are black, watery, blood-streaked, or putrid smelling, or if there are more movements than usual, then something is wrong. Fluctuations in a cat's urinary pattern may indicate changes in body chemistry. Urine should be clear yellow, not orange.

In a kitten, the eyes and nose are often first to show oncoming illness. The eyes may tear excessively, possibly with pus collecting at the inner corners; the nose may discharge either clear water or mucus.

Other signs of a sick cat include fever; prolonged vomiting; changes in appetite or water intake; excessive weight gain or loss; changes in behavior; swellings or lumps beneath the skin; abnormal discharges from body openings; hair loss, open sores, lesions, or other skin problems; prolonged sneezing or coughing; and difficulty in moving. Not all of these signs will be noticed, of course, when a cat is getting sick; certain symptoms point to one ailment, others to another. However, they are signs that should be watched for. Any one of them is enough to tell an owner that something is wrong. Don't wait to see whether the condition will correct itself. Chances are that it won't. Don't experiment with remedies suggested by well-meaning friends. Get the advice of an expert—your veterinarian. Quick action at the first sign of illness is the best shortcut to its cure.

### THE CAT'S MEDICINE CHEST

The cat's own medicine chest will be helpful to him and to you in an emergency. Put in it the things he needs or may need, items that can be found in a jiffy when illness or injury strikes: things such as sterile cotton, cotton swabs, sterile gauze dressings, 1-inch and 2-inch rolls of gauze bandage, a 1-inch roll of first aid tape, a rectal thermometer, a 3 percent solution of hydrogen peroxide to cleanse wounds, an antiseptic for minor cuts, an anti-diarrhea preparation such as Kaopectate, a liquid ant-acid such as Maalox or Pepto Bismol to treat vomiting or an upset stomach, first aid cream or antiseptic/antibacterial skin ointment such as Bacitracin for burns and abrasions, petroleum jelly, mineral oil, hairball remedy, emetic to induce vomiting in case of poisoning, flea spray or powder, and any medications that the cat usually or occasionally takes.

These are some of the supplies you may need from time to time. You will think of others. Your veterinarian can help. Even though some human remedies may be used to treat cats, keep in mind that they cannot tolerate some drugs that are helpful to people. Aspirin and aspirin substitutes, for instance, can be extremely toxic to cats, and misuse can cause weakness, vomiting, convulsions, and even death.

### QUARANTINE

When there is more than one pet in the family, a sick one should be quarantined in a separate room if such space is available. Naturally, other pets in the household will already have been exposed to the malady. The point is that the convalescing patient does not want to be disturbed by other pets or children in the family. He prefers peace and quiet.

Place the little patient's box or bed in a corner safe from drafts and shielded from strong sunlight. An even temperature—warm but not hot—and adequate ventilation—so that the air is really fresh—are desirable.

A sick cat feels the cold since he is not inclined to move about. On this account, the usual tendency is to raise the room temperature too high. The low- to mid-seventies is preferable. Additional heat, when necessary, can be supplied by placing a heating pad *under* the little one's blanket to maintain body warmth. A room too warm may render breathing more difficult where passages are clogged with mucus.

### KEEPING THE PATIENT CLEAN

Since cats are such meticulous creatures, one of the most important duties of the feline nurse is to keep the patient clean, especially when he cannot do it himself. Only when a cat is ill do we appreciate how industrious he has been in cleaning and grooming himself.

Grooming is an important part of nursing. A cat that is recovering from an illness should be groomed every other day if he is well enough. Gentle brushing or combing helps clean the skin and makes the cat less susceptible to parasites. Brushing helps distribute the hair's natural oils and, on longhairs, removes the dead hair before it has a chance to mat. Brush the hair lightly with a soft brush, or massage the skin and hair with your fingertips. This will not only make your cat look better but also make him feel more comfortable.

A light sponging with a damp washcloth is refreshing at any time of the year, especially in hot weather. If vomiting, urination, or diarrhea occurs, the hair should be sponged as soon as it becomes soiled to keep the skin from becoming irritated. Especially after diarrhea, the traces of feces that remain on the hair can harden and be difficult to remove, and, on longhairs, can form a seal over the rectum. Petroleum jelly or a mild antiseptic ointment can be daubed on the anal area to forestall irritation.

The nose and eyes should be cleaned if there is a discharge in either area. Dampen a cotton ball or washcloth with warm water and gently wipe over the face. If any matter has accumulated and caked in the eye corners or around the nostrils, soften it first with warm water, then remove the accumulation with a cotton ball (but do not rub over the eye itself with cotton—the fibers can scratch). Use a separate cotton ball around each eye.

Other aspects of cleanliness depend on how sick the cat is. The sickbed should be kept immaculate at all times. Move the litter box to the convalescent area so that the cat can quickly locate it. The weakened patient should be turned over often, not only to ease the strain of lying in one position but to prevent bed sores. If the cat cannot walk, then expect urination and bowel movements to occur in the bed. In such a case, the cat needs a softer under-bed than usual, and, since it will be soiled often, it should be of washable material. Lightweight cotton flannel blankets, cut in large squares, will do nicely because they can be laundered in the washing machine.

However soft the bedding upon which the patient lies, he will also need a wrapper or diaper. Lay under him a full-sized terry towel, disposable baby diaper, or disposable pad for pets.

### FEEDING IN ILLNESS

If your cat is recovering from an illness, the veterinarian probably will prescribe a special diet. The nutritional needs of a sick cat may differ from those of a healthy one depending on the type and severity of the illness, the cat's general condition, and the nutrients required for recovery.

Feeding in the presence of any abnormal condition often becomes a matter of getting whatever you can, whenever you can, into the little sufferer's mouth. It can be an aggravating job or a rewarding one since the appetite usually diminishes or disappears entirely throughout the period of indisposition. Sometimes the patient looks at even a favorite dish as if it disgusts him, and at other times he tries to nibble a bit as if to reward you for waiting on him.

Unless the veterinarian decrees otherwise, feed little and often of very easily digested foods. If food in a dish does not appeal, try offering small pieces from your hand. When food cannot be kept down, resort to the strained foods for babies, or nourishing bland things that are easy to digest, such as cottage cheese, beef broth, boiled eggs, and custard.

### PHONING THE VETERINARIAN

Many illnesses do not require regular visits to the veterinarian, yet he may ask to be kept informed of his patient's progress by phone. This means he will want *facts* about the pet's day-to-day condition. It is not enough to say that your cat "is about the same," or that "he seems better than he was yesterday." *Give facts*. In other words, keep a record.

Take the temperature twice daily, at ten in the morning and four in the afternoon. Watch the breathing—is it quick, strained, shallow, or is it deep, relaxed, easy? Are there muscular spasms or jerky movements, coughing, clouded eyes, unusual bowel movements, and so forth? These things can be reported accurately only when written down as you see them. So, have the record at hand when you phone the veterinarian. You will save him a lot of time, and you will stand a better chance of saving your cat.

When the veterinarian tells you what to do, do it to the letter! When medicine is to be given every two hours, that means every two hours, and in the exact amount—no more, no less. If it is a case for twenty-four-hour medication, that is, night as well as day, see that it is done. Faithful nursing has pulled many an animal through.

### RESTRAINT

In the presence of any type of indisposition, a cat's temperament may change from that of a docile, obedient pet to one definitely hostile. He may look out from beneath bed or bureau with glistening eyes seeming to say, "Come and get me if you can!" As a rule you can't, unless you dare risk being scratched or bitten.

Do not wait until the ailing cat has issued such a challenge. Before he attempts to hide, throw a towel or blanket over him. Scoop him up so that the blanket encircles his entire body (including the paws), then turn back the edge just enough to give him air. Thus restrained, you can pop him in his carrier, or transport him wherever you wish without being injured.

When it's necessary to take the temperature of or give medication to a sick cat, the owner should learn how to protect himself from bites and scratches. In most instances, a few gentle strokes and loving words will calm a frightened cat. But if your cat is hostile, and you are alone, wrap him in a towel or blanket to keep him immobilized while you give the medication. If an assistant is available, have him or her restrain the cat by grasping the loose skin on the back of the neck. Doing this should make the cat submissive. At the same time, the assistant should grab hold of the cat's hind legs with his or her other hand to prevent scratching.

Depending on what you intend to do, the assistant, still holding the cat, can then place him down on his chest or his side, or in a sitting position on a sturdy table.

### TAKING A CAT'S TEMPERATURE

Determining a cat's temperature is not difficult. It should be taken rectally, not orally, since the cat can bite down and break the thermometer.

Before inserting the rectal thermometer, hold the end between your thumb and index finger, and shake the mercury column to below 95 degrees Fahrenheit (35 degrees Celsius). Lubricate the bulb end with petroleum jelly. Place the cat on a firm surface, preferably standing with his hindquarters facing you, although the temperature can also be taken with the cat lying down.

Hold the tail up to steady the cat. Gently push almost half the length of the thermometer into the rectum, bulb end first, and hold it there for about two minutes. Then remove the thermometer, wipe it off with cotton or a tissue, and read the temperature.

A cat's normal rectal temperature is within the range

of 100.5 to 102.5 degrees Fahrenheit (38 to 39 degrees Celsius). Any elevation over 102.5 degrees Fahrenheit (39 degrees Celsius) should be considered as fever. A subnormal temperature of below 100 degrees Fahrenheit is also cause for alarm since it may indicate internal bleeding, shock, or collapse. The time of day at which the temperature is taken may affect the reading. Ordinarily, it rises in the afternoon and early evening, and drops during the morning. The temperature can also rise temporarily due to hot weather, excitement, or digestion of food, but one that *constantly remains* higher or lower than the normal range is a sign of illness.

### ADMINISTERING MEDICINES

*Pills and Capsules*—If the cat is eating well, the easiest way to give a pill or capsule is to hide it in a piece of cheese, meat, fish, or some other food he finds appetizing.

In cases where trickery doesn't work and the pill or capsule must be force-fed, coat it with butter or margarine to make it slippery. Seat the cat on a sturdy surface and have an assistant restrain him by placing both hands around his shoulders and carefully but firmly pressing downward so the cat cannot scratch with his front paws.

Gently tilt the cat's head upward. Place the palm of your hand over the cat's head. Open the mouth by pressing inward behind the canine teeth with your index finger on one side and your thumb on the other. Hold the pill between the thumb and index finger of your other hand, and use your middle finger to keep the lower jaw down. Place the pill on the cat's tongue toward the back of his throat. Close the mouth quickly and hold the jaws together as you gently stroke the cat's throat with a downward motion. If your cat is very nasty, you may have to resort to using a pill gun made for cats, a slender syringe-like device with a plunger, with which you can pop the pill into the mouth without having to put your fingers inside.

*Liquids*—Sit the cat on a firm surface and have an assistant restrain him as described above. Liquids are best poured into the corner of the mouth from a small bottle, a syringe with the needle removed, or a plastic eye dropper or medicine spoon. Gently tilt the cat's head upward. Pour the liquid, a few drops at a time, into the mouth, letting the cat swallow it before giving more.

*Eye Medication*—Eye medication usually comes in liquid or ointment form. To apply liquid, tilt the cat's head upward. Hold the container between your thumb and index finger, steadying the palm of this hand on the cat's head. The prescribed amount of medication can then be dropped into the corner of the eye(s). To apply ointment, gently tilt the cat's head upward. Pull the lower lid downward, and squeeze a little ointment on the inside. Let the lid go back into place, and, when the cat blinks his eyelids, the medication will coat the entire eye.

*Ear Medication*—Ear medication also comes in liquid or ointment form. Hold the ear flap carefully. Insert the required amount of liquid or ointment into the ear canal. Steady the cat's head with your hand to keep him from shaking while you massage the base of the ear to spread the medication inside. Release your hold on the head.

# 13
# Breeding and Reproduction

It is not unusual for members of a kindhearted family to become breeders almost overnight. You may not have the slightest intention of breeding kittens, but fate decides otherwise. It happens now and then!

One fine morning a forlorn little stranger waits on your doorstep. You bring her in, feed her, warm her until as the weeks go by, she grows sleek and plump as an oyster. Then a neighbor tips you off: you have inherited a pregnant queen. Accepting your responsibilities with good grace, you give the stranger every care.

Of course the prospective breeding picture may be entirely different, as when you own a pedigreed, registered queen and plan to breed her and raise kittens. In either case, you will need to understand the principles and practices of feline reproduction explained in this chapter.

### WHEN DO CATS REACH SEXUAL MATURITY?

Both female and male cats show an uninhibited interest in sex at an early age. The female cat (queen) reaches sexual maturity within six to ten months, during which time she will start coming into "heat." You will have no trouble knowing when the season occurs, for the queen herself will announce it by rubbing against objects, rolling around on the floor, emitting vocal "calls," and making herself something of a nuisance to show that she's ready to breed.

The male cat (tom), although capable of amorous urges by six months of age, usually reaches sexual maturity between nine and twelve months. While female cats can be bred only when they are in season, males can (and do) mate at any time.

### THE AGE TO BREED

Female cats should be physically and mentally mature before they are bred. If your queen is between six and ten months old when she has her first season, it is wise to wait until she is at least a year old before breeding her. If she has her first season at twelve months of age or later, she may be bred, providing that she is mature. It depends on the particular queen. If you are confused, seek your veterinarian's advice about the correct age to breed.

### THE QUEEN IN HEAT

Unlike female dogs, that go into heat semiannually, queens are polyestrous animals, which means that they experience many heat periods over the course of a year. The number of heat periods and their frequency depend on the time of year as well as the nature of each cat. In this country, they tend to start in January or February and extend through August and September. Most queens do not cycle between October and December; but there are exceptions, and some cycle year round. Other factors that can affect the queen's reproductive cycle include environmental temperature, increased periods of daylight, and close proximity to tomcats and other cycling queens.

A heat period lasts about four to seven days if the queen is bred. If she is not bred, the heat lasts at least ten days and recurs at regular intervals. Some queens are constantly in heat during breeding season if they are not mated. Owners will have to breed them, or have ovulation induced by a veterinarian to shorten the heat period, or have them spayed.

Basically, reproductive behavior in cats is comparable to that of other mammals with one exception that involves the female's ovulation process. Most mammals, including humans, are "spontaneous" ovulators, which means that, whether bred or not, they can produce ova or eggs. The felids are different: They are "induced" ovulators, meaning that they will ovulate only when stimulated to do so, either by the penis during mating or by artificial stimulation.

The queen's heat cycle basically has several phases: *Proestrus* is the beginning stage, which lasts about one to three days and causes behavioral changes. The queen will become extremely affectionate and start rubbing persistently against her owner's feet, the furniture, or other objects. She may start to cry a little and lift her tail and elevate her hindquarters. She may permit a male to approach her, but attempts to mate will only arouse her anger.

Then the queen enters *estrus,* or the stage of true heat, during which she will permit mating. She'll rub frantically and "call" out to males in her distinct mating cry. Her pituitary gland produces a hormone that stimulates the growth of tiny follicles in her ovaries that contain immature eggs. The ovarian follicles also produce the female hormone estrogen.

If the queen's vagina is stimulated during mating by the barblike spines on the tom's penis, her pituitary gland releases a luteinizing hormone that triggers the egg-releasing process known as ovulation. Then the ovarian follicles release progesterone, a female hormone that prepares the uterus for fertilized eggs and maintains pregnancy.

If the cat does not ovulate, the heat period lasts at least ten days and recurs at approximately fourteen- to twenty-one-day intervals. If a cat is continuously in heat, she may be artificially stimulated to induce ovulation, but this should only be done by a veterinarian. After ovulation, the queen will complete her cycle and not come into heat again for about forty-five to sixty days. Some queens that are artificially stimulated to ovulate, however, go through false pregnancies.

#### FALSE PREGNANCY

If ovulation occurs by artificial stimulation and no eggs are fertilized, a false pregnancy (or pseudo-pregnancy) may follow. This frequently occurs when, during ovulation, the pregnancy hormone progesterone is released even though a natural breeding has not taken place.

The signs of false pregnancy are barely noticeable in some queens and very apparent in others. Physical signs generally appear in about three to four weeks and range from a slight swelling of the breasts with a mild watery secretion, to noticeable abdominal swelling and enlarged breasts that produce milk. Emotionally, the queen may act as though she were pregnant—preparing a "nest" for her kittens, sleeping more, eating more, and trying to hide in secluded places. She may be quite restless and believe that one of her toys or some other soft object is her kitten. She will carry it around and act very possessively toward the object.

If the symptoms of false pregnancy are not severe, the queen usually recovers from this state within a week or so. If the signs are severe, consult your veterinarian as soon as possible. He may recommend hormone treatment or suggest having her spayed.

### ARRANGING THE BREEDING

If your queen is a purebred and you plan to register her kittens, the choice of a stud tom requires a great deal of study and consideration. He should be selected well in advance of mating time. It is best to choose an experienced stud—especially if your female has never been mated—whose bloodlines complement those of your queen and whose virtues exceed her faults. No cat is perfect. The object should be to produce offspring, through selective breeding, that are better than their parents.

The owner of the stud will want to know all about your female and will ask to see her pedigree. You'll probably be asked to produce a health certificate, proof of current vaccinations, and possibly a certificate indicating that she is free from feline leukemia virus. Don't be offended. You have the right, of course, to ask the stud's owner for similar documents.

The owner of the stud receives some type of payment for the male's services. Usually, it is a cash fee, payable at the time of mating. Purebred stud fees start at around $100 and can go much higher depending on the cat's record as a sire and show winner. Sometimes the owner may waive the fee and agree to take "pick of the litter." Giving up the choice kitten can be risky, especially if there is only one kitten—or one extraordinary kitten in an otherwise average litter. You'll have to give it up! Complications and misunderstandings can and do occur. Whatever type of payment is agreed upon, it is important to record all the facts in an informal contract to be signed by both owners.


### TAKING THE QUEEN TO THE STUD

After picking a suitable stud for your queen, you will need to make a conditional appointment for his services. It is nearly impossible to determine exactly when your queen will come into heat, but you probably can estimate the approximate date by reviewing her prior seasons. At the first signs of proestrus, you should phone the owner of the stud and arrange to deliver your queen.

Territory is extremely important to the tom's sexual behavior, and for this reason, the queen goes to the stud, in most instances, because he feels more secure in familiar quarters. You should deliver your queen, confined in a sturdy carrier, to the stud. Make sure you take her health and vaccination certificates with you. If you cannot take the queen to the stud and have to ship her unaccompanied by air, make travel arrangements promptly, then confirm them with the stud's owners so they can collect her as soon as she arrives. A long journey often unsettles a queen; she may stop calling by the time she reaches her destination and may have to board there until she comes back into heat.

Upon arrival, the queen will be checked to make sure that she is in good health. Then she will be placed in separate quarters near the tom where she can settle in. Here, she can adjust to her new surroundings and become acquainted with the tom on the other side of the wire mesh.

## COURTSHIP AND BREEDING

Once the queen starts making advances to the stud, the owner will let her join the stud in his own quarters or in a breeding area. There, an elaborate courtship takes place that can last up to several minutes.

Although each tom has his own way of courting a queen, generally there is a pattern to the proceedings. The male usually begins by circling the queen and then approaching her. She often repels the tom's advances by hissing and clawing. The male usually backs off, then cries out to her and resumes his advances a few moments later. The queen purrs and may roll on her back in front of her mate, or the pair may investigate each other through mutual sniffing. The stud may lick the queen's face and then try to inspect her vulva.

All these actions stimulate the queen, and she soon assumes the characteristic mating position—body bent low to the ground with hindquarters raised, hind legs apart, and tail swung to one side—while the male prepares to mount her.

The tom then mounts the queen and holds the scruff of her neck between his teeth. He encircles her body with his front legs and his hind legs, and begins to make thrusting motions as his penis becomes erect. At the same time, the queen makes stepping movements with her hind feet to expedite insertion. After several rapid thrusts by the stud in which penetration occurs, the tom ejaculates in a few seconds while the queen utters a shrill howl. She will pull away, turn toward the tom, and spit and scratch at him.

Once the tom has withdrawn, the queen rolls and rubs sensuously on the floor. Both partners will lick their genitals. Within fifteen to sixty minutes later, depending on the queen, the mating sequence begins again and may be repeated many times a day. A minimum of three observed matings is suggested to assure the chances of conception.

When your queen returns home, keep her confined in the house as she may still be in estrus. Female felines are "superfecund," which means that each of the kittens in her litter can have a different father. Do not let her run free: She could have some eggs fertilized by the sperm of the chosen purebred stud, and other eggs fertilized by the sperm of an alley cat!

If the queen did not conceive, she will start calling again within three to four weeks, and you will have to return her to the stud. If she did conceive, you can expect the kittens to arrive in approximately nine weeks. The gestation period, or interval from the time of mating to the birth of the kittens, lasts sixty-three days more or less.

### CARE DURING PREGNANCY

Whether the mother-to-be is a purebred or an abandoned waif picked up off the street, her care is much the same. In addition to providing her with comfortable surroundings and lots of affection, keep the queen on her normal routine and diet for the first three weeks after mating. All external parasites, such as fleas and ear mites, should be eliminated at this time. The first sign of pregnancy occurs around the third week, when the nipples start to enlarge and turn pink.

Feed the queen nutritious food during pregnancy, as well as a vitamin and mineral supplement. Your veterinarian can advise you about diet and supplements. The queen's appetite will begin to increase around the fourth week, and you should gradually enlarge her food intake. Foods that contain high protein levels (meat, fish, poultry, cooked eggs, and cheese) and milk, plus a choice commercial cat food, are especially nutritious.

Between the sixth and seventh weeks, the queen's abdomen will become noticeably swollen. Throughout pregnancy, the queen does need exercise, and she should be encouraged to run about the house and play as she likes. She should not be allowed to jump from high places, however, and children should not lift her, since any fall could cause her to miscarry.

During the last weeks of pregnancy, as the queen's size increases, she may not be able to eat large meals. It will be far easier on her digestion to divide her food intake into several smaller meals each day.

Because of her increased size, the queen may not be able to groom herself satisfactorily. Comb and brush her every day to remove dead hair and to keep her skin in good condition. Don't put a potentially harmful substance on her coat that could be licked off. Should she become infested with fleas or ear mites at this late date, seek your veterinarian's advice. Do not give the queen any medication or vaccines during her pregnancy unless you have been told to do so by your veterinarian.

### PREPARING FOR DELIVERY

As delivery time approaches, the queen will become restless and start searching through all the secluded places in your house for a place to give birth to her kittens. It makes good sense to prepare a kittening box deep enough to shield the matron from drafts, but not so deep that she has to strain to leap into it. A large corrugated box will do, preferably one with a cutout for a front entrance. Line the box with several thicknesses of newspaper and cover these with a washable cotton blanket. (Once the kittens are born, provide an additional blanket to throw over the top to keep the babies warm through the night.) Place the box in a warm, draft-free area, away from children, other pets, and the family's normal traffic pattern. As soon as the box is ready, introduce the queen to it. If she has enough time to get used to the box, she will choose it for her kittening instead of trying to hide her young ones in some inaccessible place.

A smaller box or kitten bed is often made ready and placed close beside the mother's box so that, during the birth of the litter, each one can be kept safe and warm while the queen is busy giving birth to the next one.

You should also have on hand a few other items you may need for the delivery: a rectal thermometer, several freshly laundered towels, paper toweling or other porous materials, petroleum or lubricating jelly, dental floss or white nylon thread, an antiseptic safe for cats, blunt-tipped scissors, and cotton balls.

As the delivery date approaches, the prospective mother is less active and she may sleep a lot. By the ninth week, she becomes restless and usually starts rearranging the bedding in her box. Let her do this, but when actual labor begins, remove the blanket and put down paper towels, newspapers, or other absorbent material to soak up the discharges from the delivery.

Notify your veterinarian during the end of the eighth week that delivery is imminent. Most queens have no trouble giving birth, and veterinary assistance is rarely required; but it's good to know that help is available if you need it. If the queen has long hair, delivery will be more sanitary if you *carefully* trim away some of the fur around the vulva, the anus, and the breasts. You can help the queen keep those areas clean by sponging them with a little warm water and mild soap, rinsing, and then drying them thoroughly.

## THE FIRST SIGNS OF LABOR

There are no hard rules controlling the length of labor. The queen may deliver a litter of four kittens in less than two hours, or she may take six hours or longer. When labor starts, the queen will become progressively restless. She will refuse to eat. She will roam around the house and go in and out of her box, frantically rearranging its contents. She may lick herself constantly and will urinate frequently; in fact, the queen may interrupt her normal activities to rush to the litter tray.

She may start breathing rapidly and panting. Her vulva will become soft and swollen, and as labor progresses, there will be a discharge from the vagina, colorless at first, and then blood tinged. If the discharge is very bloody, greenish colored, or foul smelling, *notify your veterinarian immediately*. This may indicate a decomposed fetus or detached placenta.

One way to determine that labor is beginning is by monitoring the queen's body temperature. Normally, it is in the range of 100.5 to 102.5 degrees Fahrenheit. When it drops below 100 degrees Fahrenheit and stays at this lower level without fluctuating, it signifies that delivery should occur within twenty-four hours.

### THE DELIVERY

The next phase of labor begins when the queen's abdominal muscles begin to contract. As she lies on her side, you will be able to see and feel the contractions. These force the kittens down the birth canal. The queen will pant, lick her vulva repeatedly, and bear down, trying to expel the fetuses.

Soon, her vaginal opening will dilate, and the first transparent sac—the membrane that surrounds each kitten—will come into view. After a few hard contractions, the queen should push out the sac.

As soon as the sac is expelled, the queen should turn around and tear it open with her teeth and start to lick the kitten. Her licking stimulates the kitten's respiratory and circulatory systems to function, and soon it will begin to move and perhaps cry. Next the queen will bite off the umbilical cord about an inch or so from the kitten's navel.

Should an inexperienced queen fail to perform these actions, she'll have to be helped. If the membrane is covering the newborn kitten, carefully break it open with your fingers, releasing the head first to prevent suffocation. Wipe away any mucus from the kitten's mouth and nostrils, then massage it with a warm towel. Next, you should carefully attend to the umbilical cord. Tie a piece of dental floss (or cotton thread) around the cord about an inch or so from the kitten's navel. Cut the cord in front of the knotted thread, then swab the severed edge with antiseptic.

Once the first kitten has emerged, the afterbirth, or placenta, usually follows. The queen may try to eat the afterbirth when it appears. Many mammals do this instinctively, probably to remove material that could attract predators. Don't let her eat more than one or two afterbirths, however, because consuming too many may give her diarrhea. There will be one afterbirth for each kitten. Be sure they are all expelled; any retained placental matter can cause infection.

After the kitten is breathing adequately, it should be placed next to its mother. A healthy kitten will soon find her teats and begin to nurse. If it does not, gently squeeze a little milk from one of her breasts and put the kitten's mouth around it.

The actions previously described will be repeated with the birth of each kitten. The time between each birth will vary: It can range from as few as ten or fifteen minutes to as long as two hours in a normal delivery. The average litter numbers four kittens. After each delivery, you can offer the queen a drink or a little bit of her favorite food.

### DANGER SIGNS DURING DELIVERY

Queens rarely have problems giving birth; however, if any of the following signs are apparent, call your veterinarian immediately:

- Your queen has been straining *forcefully* for more than one hour without delivering a kitten. This may indicate two kittens blocking the birth canal, or kittens too large to pass through the birth canal. Sometimes a Caesarian section is necessary.
- The queen tires before a kitten is born, or her con-

tractions weaken or stop completely although she is obviously still carrying kittens. This is an indication of uterine inertia.
- The queen screams in agony as she strains to expel a kitten.

### POSTNATAL CARE

Once the entire litter has arrived, remove the soiled papers from the delivery box and put down a fresh supply. Encourage the mother to go to the litter box for relief. When she returns, she will curl up around her babies to keep them warm and to give them easy access to her nipples. Ordinarily the tiny newcomers are expert in finding the nipples to begin nursing, but be sure they do find them. The queen's first milk, a watery secretion called "colostrum," is rich in proteins and minerals, and contains antibodies that grant the kittens immunity from certain infectious diseases.

Feed the queen as much soft and bland food as she desires for the first day or two, plus plenty of fresh water, then return her to her regular diet, supplemented by the high-protein foods added during pregnancy. Feed the new mother as much as she wants to eat during the nursing period. Lactation is a crucial period during which the queen requires increased levels of food. And if you do not give her adequate nourishment, she will use up her own body reserves feeding her growing kittens.

### DANGER SIGNS AFTER DELIVERY

Call your veterinarian immediately if you notice any of the following signs after delivery of the kittens:

- The queen expels a foul-smelling or greenish discharge. This may indicate a retained placenta.
- The queen bleeds profusely from the vagina.
- The queen is feverish.
- The kittens are restless and cry continually. This may mean the queen has no milk.
- The queen's breasts are distended and discolored.

### CARING FOR THE KITTENS

For the first few weeks after the delivery, there is little to do except keep the queen supplied with lots of nutritious food. Examine her every day to see that her abdomen and rectum are clean and that her breasts are not caked with milk. If she has long hair, you may have to sponge and dry her underparts to keep the hair from becoming sticky and matted while the kittens are nursing.

The kittens are born utterly helpless. They cannot see or hear. All they can recognize is the warmth of their mother's breasts as they nuzzle up to her to nurse for short periods of time day and night. Their only strength consists of pushing with their feet and grasping the nipples to suck. You should check to see that each kitten is nursing properly and growing as rapidly as the others.

The senses of smell and taste are acquired in a few days; the eyes, tightly shut at birth, open between the seventh and tenth days, but time must elapse before they can focus and really see. Newly opened eyes are sensitive to glare, and the box should be kept out of direct sunlight. During the second week, the ears break their seals and the little babies can hear. During the fourth week, the baby teeth begin to come in, and the kittens start toddling around their box. By the fifth week, they are standing firmly on their feet and playing with their littermates. You'll see them leaping, arching their backs, and stalking each other. Longhaired kittens should receive a little daily grooming so they learn to accept this procedure when their hair grows longer and their care becomes more time-consuming.

To determine the sex of the kittens, look under the tail. You will see that the females have two dots or openings, and the males three. Examine a few kittens together and it should not be too difficult to verify their sex.

Mother cats know instinctively the care their young ones require. They are naturally efficient mothers, ready and willing to nurse their brood for a full eight weeks and occasionally longer when their milk supply holds out. They wash their kittens a dozen times a day and clean up after them as often as required. By cuddling them up in a heap against their breasts, they see to it that the kittens are kept warm, and they hitch themselves adroitly around a crying baby to make sure it can reach their milk-filled nipples.

Between the fourth and fifth weeks, the kittens will benefit from supplemental feeding. They may be offered warm milk to lap, or a little beef broth. Valuable, too, are tiny tastes of ground beef. Exactly when semisolid and solid foods are introduced for the first time differs from litter to litter, but as a rule, supplementary feeding may begin when the baby teeth break through the gums— between the fourth and fifth weeks. Around this time, be sure to check with your veterinarian about early immunization.

### FEEDING

The menu at five weeks may consist of nursing as usual and two or three drinks of milk for the kittens to lap from a shallow dish during the day. Cow's milk, goat's milk, or a kitten milk substitute will very likely be relished once it has been hesitatingly tasted. But take care: Avoid mixing different kinds of milk. Stick to the same kind, at least while the kittens are very young.

You may add baby cereal or a finely shredded commercial kitten food to the milk at this time, mixing it to a soupy consistency. After a few days you can add a little strained baby food, ground beef, chopped chicken, salmon, canned cat food, or other soft solid food. Liquify all meats or canned food in a blender at first; then as soon as the kittens are eating well, thicken the food's consistency.

Foods offered at six weeks are practically the same as during the previous week, only the amount is increased as the little ones grow. This means nursing as usual and one meal a day, then two, and then three—until the kittens are completely weaned by seven to eight weeks of age. It is advisable to keep the babies away from the queen during the day to rest her and to stimulate the kittens' appetite for solid food.

It must be kept in mind that the transition from liquid to solid food may be difficult in some cases for the digestive processes to handle. Changes in diet are best made slowly and carefully—never abruptly. Avoid trying more than one new food each day. Go slowly and let the stomach learn its new job without shock.

Regularity in feeding is as important at this stage as it is in later life. The baby stomach, it seems, always needs something to work on. In the nest the kittens are forever nursing, a little at a time. So throughout the gradual weaning period, which may last from their fourth to eighth weeks, it is important to see that their ever-present hunger is satisfied.

Three feedings per day of supplementary food will

be about right as long as the mother's breasts are handy for between-meal snacks; but when she is taken from the kittens by day, four or even five meals will be needed. As time goes on, the increased amounts of dish feeding will dull the appetite for mother's milk, at least to some degree, and the queen without doubt will be more than willing to shift the entire responsibility for this service to somebody else.

## INTRODUCING THE LITTER BOX

If a litter box is placed in or near the kittens' box, they will learn to use it, usually with a little encouragement from their mother. You can reinforce her training by placing each kitten in the tray several times a day, especially after feeding.

## THE TEMPORARY TEETH

Eruption of the temporary or milk teeth around the fourth week of age apparently causes the kittens little concern. The teeth are quite tiny, hence they break through the gums early. Jaw strength at this age does not amount to much, but the little ones do increase it as they grab their littermates in play and needle their mother's breasts as they nurse. She submits to this needling as long as she can, but soon you will find her jumping up as if to complain about the pain. You can almost hear her say, "That's about enough; I've had it!" as she proceeds to leave the box and spend more time away from her brood.

The care of kittens in the nest may sound complicated, but actually it is just plain common sense. The queen provides the kittens with food and warmth until the teeth come in, and she cleans her babies constantly. Reluctantly, she leaves them at intervals to go outside or to her litter box—in fact, she almost has to be pried loose. Then, when the teeth erupt, the breeder serves the simple meals suggested above.

### PREVENTING PREGNANCY: SPAYING AND NEUTERING

If you do not want to breed your cat after she or he reaches sexual maturity, you should consider spaying or neutering. "Spaying" a female and "neutering" a male are terms that describe the surgical procedures to remove the reproductive organs.

Spaying is then the only permanent answer to recurring heat periods or unwanted pregnancies in a queen. The procedure involves the removal of both ovaries, the uterus, and cervix under general anesthesia. The best time to spay is between six and seventh months of age, before the female has experienced her first heat. The operation can be performed at any age as long as the female is in good health and not grossly overweight; but the longer you postpone it, the more serious it becomes. The operation, called an ovariohysterectomy, involves an abdominal incision with sutures (these usually are removed in a follow-up visit), and an overnight stay at the veterinary hospital. Once the cat returns home, she should be kept warm and quiet for a few days. She should not be allowed to pull at her stitches, and her activities should be restrained until the sutures are removed.

The best time to neuter a male cat is when he is about nine months of age: after he has become sexually mature, but before he has a chance to develop bad habits. The operation, called an orchiectomy, can be performed at any age, but the sooner it is done after sexual maturity, the better. The surgery involves a general anesthesia, the removal of the testicles, the tying of the spermatic cords, and an overnight stay at the hospital.

The cost of the surgical procedure depends on the size, sex, age, and health of the cat. Many communities, concerned about the overpopulation of cats and dogs, offer low-cost or nonprofit spay/neuter clinics. Whatever the cost, it's much cheaper than caring for unwanted litters!

Birth control is just one of the benefits of spaying and neutering. The procedures make cats of both sexes more gentle and affectionate and less aggressive. Females will not experience the heat cycle, which puts an end to vaginal discharges and the swarm of noisy suitors that camp on their doorsteps when they are in heat. Males are less likely to roam in search of females, which reduces the risk of fights or other injuries. Neutering usually stops the repulsive habit of spraying urine to mark territories.

Best of all, spayed and neutered cats usually live longer and healthier lives. Studies show that spaying eliminates the possibilities of uterine disease, such as pyrometra and cancer, and reduces the risk of breast tumors. Males have a reduced risk of prostate cancer.

# 14
# Traveling and Shipping

Taking a cat along on a journey can be easy or difficult. It all depends on whether traveling is a new experience or merely another way of getting around for which the pet has been trained. The trip may be long or short; the conveyance a car, a bus, a train, or a plane. Whichever it is, preparation for the journey is much the same if the cat is not to be frightened out of his wits and the owner so exasperated that he says *never again!*

Advanced training for travel of any kind is often neglected. "Our cat is strictly a homebody," you say. "He does not need to travel." But the time is bound to come when he must be transported, even if only around the block, under perfect control.

Frequent or at least occasional trips to the veterinary hospital are necessary. And fires, hurricanes, floods, and earthquakes are no rarity; they come without warning, and frequently small animals must be evacuated together with their owners. The noise and excitement of such catastrophes cannot be taken in stride by any pet.

## THE CARRIER

You may have on hand a small cardboard carrier in which you brought your kitten home. This can be used for the occasional trip to the veterinarian, but it is not sturdy enough for long journeys. Most pet stores carry a variety of wicker, vinyl, or high density polyethylene traveling cases for cats. Choose one with a secure latch that is roomy enough for your cat to stand up or stretch out in, has a leakproof bottom, and is well ventilated, chew-resistant, and easy to clean.

Place a towel or lightweight blanket on the floor of the case. Attach a label clearly marked with your name and address to the handle. Do not depend on borrowing someone else's carrier; it may not be available when you need it, and, if it is accessible, it may not be clean and germ free. In short, a sturdy carrier, kept ready and waiting, will go a long way toward contributing to your cat's safe and comfortable journey.

## INTRODUCING YOUR CAT TO HIS CARRIER

The next step is to accustom your cat to the carrier. Place it in a conspicuous place, open the door or lid, put a favorite toy inside, and let him go in and out at will for a few days. You could also try to entice the cat into the carrier with a few treats. Let him sleep in the carrier if he likes, or allow him to use it for occasional naps during the day, with the door or top alternately opened or closed. Begin this training as early in life as possible so your cat will accept his carrier as a secure place in which to relax.

Get your cat used to being carried around in the carrier—first in the house, then around the block, and finally in the car. Talk reassuringly to him as you go, let him see you through the ventilation panels, and in no time at all he will learn that this is a comfortable way to be moved about.

These preliminary steps are the most important phase of travel schooling. You will certainly realize this in an emergency, should you have to stuff the little fellow into a strange carrying case and he becomes so frightened that he tries to claw and bite holes in it. You may decide to enter him for competition in a cat show, too, and you do not want him to arrive nervous and bedraggled. Once thoroughly trained to his own carrier, a cat arrives at his destination in as good condition as when he left home.

### PREPARING FOR A JOURNEY

A little advance planning will help make your cat more comfortable en route. If you are traveling to another state, consult your veterinarian a few weeks before your trip to ascertain that your cat has all his necessary vaccinations. Most states require a health certificate and proof of rabies vaccination. If your cat goes along with you in the car, you probably will never have to produce these certificates; but if you are traveling by plane, most airlines will ask for them before accepting a pet.

Feed your cat a light meal about four hours before the trip, then give him only a few sips of water before setting out.

Don't forget a litter box for your cat. Most pet stores sell small, disposable cardboard litter boxes; these are inexpensive and excellent for travel. If you'll be away overnight or longer, take along a supply of food and the cat's food and water dishes. Pack enough food for the entire trip, and avoid changes in diet. Feeding new food can cause digestive upsets. You might want to pack a container of water from home as well. Changes in drinking water can also upset digestion.

## TRAVEL BY CAR

The majority of cats learn to be good automobile riders with no trouble at all; the comparatively few timid ones can be taught to ride comfortably if certain preliminaries are observed. It is a mistake to wait until departure time and learn that problems exist. The trick is to let your cat gain experience in gradual stages, so that when you do have to make a long journey, he will be an expert traveler.

The first goal is to take your cat to and from the car safely. You can do this either by putting a collar or harness on the cat, attaching a leash and holding it tightly in your hand, or by putting the cat in his carrier. *Never* carry an unleashed cat in your arms. A loud noise can frighten him and make him jump out of your arms and run away.

Once inside the car, you must still be concerned about the cat's safety. Keep the cat under control by not removing his collar and leash, by letting him sit on someone's lap, or by keeping him confined in his carrier. Uncontrolled cats are a danger in a moving vehicle:They can jump out of an open window, they can leap from the back seat to the front and confuse the driver, they can crawl under the dashboard or around the driver's feet and cause an accident by pushing down the accelerator or brake. When the cat is enclosed in his carrier, place it on the car seat to minimize jolt and sideway. If the carrier must be stored on the floor for lack of room, it will perhaps be less disturbed by motion if it is underlaid with a foam rubber pillow.

Begin the schooling with short drives: through the

neighborhood, or to drop off the children at school. Each time you stop, *be sure the cat is held firmly on leash or confined in his carrier before you open a window or a door*. After a few trips, your cat should begin to accept road travel.

Cats usually do not become carsick as often as dogs, but a few remain poor travelers in spite of all we do to help them. Depending on the problem, ask your veterinarian to prescribe a motion-sickness preparation or a tranquilizer.

### STAYING IN HOTELS AND MOTELS

Gaines Professional Services publishes *Touring with Towser*, a 64-page directory of motels and hotels in the United States and Canada that accept pets. Send $1.50 to Gaines *Touring with Towser*, P.O. Box 1007, Kankakee, Illinois 60901.

When you stay in a hotel or motel, the carrier is invaluable as a safe sleeping place. Left free to roam the room at night, a cat may try to escape out a window while his owners sleep—in fact when pets share your bedroom, no window should ever be opened from the bottom. Furthermore, when nestled comfortably in his carrier, a cat cannot amuse himself manicuring his nails by clawing furniture and draperies for which you may be billed by the management.

We sometimes scoff at hotel managers who prohibit pets on their premises. We think they don't like animals. But various proprietors have had many experiences of rooms left in shambles by pets allowed to do as they please. Such complaints are growing less with time as pet owners realize their responsibilities in keeping rented quarters clean and claw-free. Observing a few precautions will make your cat welcome in most hotels and motels.

Bring along a supply of polyethylene garbage bags. Line the wastebaskets with them before you dispose of empty cat food cans or change the litter. Pack an old towel or bath mat to put beneath the litter box. If your cat tracks litter out of the box, keep the room clean by shaking it back inside. And if your cat is leash-trained, ask the management where he may be walked. Avoid going near swimming pools, flower gardens, or the beach.

The carrying case will keep your cat from escaping should the family rent a seaside cottage for the summer. The rented home, like the hotel and motel, must be protected against serious damage by animal occupants. The farsighted car owner takes with him an old blanket or a few sheets or other coverings to throw over chairs and sofas, familiar toys to prevent boredom, maybe even a familiar scratching post, and certainly a litter box with plenty of fresh litter.

### LEAVING CATS IN PARKED CARS

Stealing animals from parked cars is not unusual these days. Even when the car is locked, thieves break in and take whatever they can lay their hands on. So if you stop en route, try to take the carrier with you.

When you must leave the cat alone in the car, however, park in a well-shaded area. Open the window slightly for ventilation, but not enough for the cat to escape if he's loose inside. Check the car frequently in hot weather, and return as fast as you can. A car in direct sunlight gets hot inside very quickly; in a matter of minutes, interior temperatures can reach 110 degrees Fahrenheit.

## TRAVELING BY BUS, SUBWAY, AND TRAIN

On most local buses and subways, cats will not be objected to provided they are safely latched in a carrier. Don't, however, make the mistake of thinking that you can fool the driver and take your four-footed companion out of the carrier to let him ride on your lap! Aside from guide dogs for the blind, Trailways, Greyhound, and other interstate bus lines do not accept pets.

Amtrak, which provides nationwide rail service, stopped accepting pets in both the passenger and baggage compartments in 1977 when a new U.S. government regulation established strict guidelines for space and temperature requirements. Via Rail, which serves all of Canada, will accept cats—confined in carriers—in the baggage sections of some but not all trains. Some smaller American and Canadian railroads also accept cats, but they almost always have to ride in the luggage compartments.

## TRAVELING BY PLANE

Air travel is probably the best of all possible methods of long-distance traveling because the cat is in transit a much shorter time. Most cats travel well by air, but it can be risky to send a cat that is pregnant, in season, very old, or in poor health on a long flight.

Airlines have specific rules about the shipment of animals, and these generally conform to the regulations laid down by the International Air Transport Association (IATA). Some airlines will allow one or two pets to travel with their owners in the passenger section of a plane. The pet must be small enough, however, to fit into a carrier about twelve inches square that will slide under the seat. Otherwise, the cat must travel in a special pressurized and heated area in the cargo section. In either case, it is wise to make reservations in advance.

If your cat is able to go with you in the passenger cabin, you can purchase directly from the airline an inexpensive, small carrying case that fits under the seat. If the cat has to go in the cargo section, he must travel in a sturdy shipping container that meets air travel regulations. (See below, "Shipping Your Cat," for more information.)

Feed your cat a light meal and a drink about four hours before the trip. If the cat is nervous, you can administer (under veterinary supervision) a mild tranquilizer. Don't forget to take along your cat's health certificate and other necessary documents.

### SHIPPING YOUR CAT

Shipping a cat destined to go to a new home is a serious matter, and every precaution must be taken for his comfort and safety.

Several details should be arranged before the departure date. The first is to see that the cat's vaccinations are current. If they are not, visit your veterinarian promptly. The next step is to schedule a *direct* flight from the point of origin to the point of destination. If that isn't possible, pick the flight with the least number of stops. Avoid shipping toward the end of the week when potential holdovers may lengthen the journey even more. And avoid trips during very hot or very cold weather. Unfortunately, the quality of service varies from one airport to another, and pets in shipping crates have been observed occasionally sitting in direct sunlight, rain, and snow on the tarmac between flights.

Don't forget to give the new owner the name of the airline carrying the cat, the flight number, the name of the airport, and the estimated time of arrival.

For such journeys, a strong crate that meets air travel regulations is necessary. Briefly, a shipping container should be:

1. Roomy enough for an animal to stand up, turn around, and lie down in with normal posture and body movements.
2. Solidly constructed with a door made to prevent accidental opening. (See that the top of the crate is solid, so that nothing can fall through.) The container should have a leakproof bottom, and the joints should be snugly fitted so there is no chance of the pet escaping.
3. Free of interior protrusions that could injure the animal.
4. Ventilated adequately on at least two opposite walls. At least one-third of the ventilation area must be in the lower half of the container, and one-third in the upper half, so that air can flow through both parts.
5. Fitted with a rim or other projecting device on the outside of the ventilated area to prevent the openings from being blocked by adjacent cargo.
6. Fitted with sturdy handles or grips.
7. Marked on the top and at least one side with the words LIVE ANIMAL in letters not less than one inch high, and with arrows indicating the upright position.

On the day of departure, put the cat's health certificates and other important documents in a heavy manila envelope marked IMPORTANT PAPERS, and tape it securely to the top of the carrier. Attach clearly printed labels with the new owner's name, address, and telephone number. If the trip will be lengthy, include dry food in a Ziploc plastic bag complete with feeding instructions. Make sure the carrier has a dish that can be filled without opening the door. Don't fill it with food or water before the trip: the contents will only spill. Put some shredded newspaper in the bottom of the carrier to absorb urine.

You will be instructed to bring the cat to the airport several hours before the scheduled departure time. If possible, stay at the airport until the flight leaves. Otherwise leave your name and telephone number with the freight agent and ask to be notified if the flight is delayed or canceled.

## BOARDING YOUR CAT

There may come a time when you must travel alone and leave your cat at home. This is a problem that confronts many pet owners at one time or another; in fact, it sometimes becomes a psychological problem that keeps people from traveling at all. They fear placing their cats in the care of strangers—"he won't eat for anyone but me, he won't sleep except on my bed, he'll grieve his heart out and be nothing but skin and bones when we get back . . ."

Such an attitude is natural when one becomes attached to a pet, but it is foolish to let it assume such proportions. The pet that chains his owner to the home is usually one that has been denied a reasonable amount of experience in normal living. He probably has been so overprotected that he has never grown up! Association with other people and places gives him savoir faire that comes in handy when he does have to leave his own folks behind.

Where do you leave your cat when you go away: with a relative or a reliable friend, at a boarding cattery or kennel, or with the veterinarian?

The reliable relative or friend probably has the time to care for the cat to make him feel at home but may not have the proper facilities or equipment to keep the little stranger from wandering away. It is possible, though, to locate a professional cat sitter who will live in your home while you are away.

The boarding cattery or boarding kennel (the latter handles both dogs and cats) has the necessary facilities, equipment, and professional staff to ensure a pet's safety and comfort. You can locate such establishments in the classified telephone directory, or by asking for recommendations from your veterinarian or from friends who have cats that have been favorably boarded.

The veterinarian, too, has all the equipment needed to safeguard a cat and keep him comfortable. Most veterinarians accept a few boarders as a convenience only, so they are not apt to be overcrowded. And usually they separate the healthy animals from the ailing ones. This is important. While the veterinarian is too busy to give much personal attention to each boarder, he has expert assistants keeping an eye out for the slightest signs of subnormal conditions.

Arrangements for boarding should be made well in advance. Capable boarding establishments are heavily booked, especially during the summer months or on weekends or holidays. If this is your cat's first trip away from home, ask if you can bring along some of his favorite things—a few toys, his blanket or basket—to make the adjustment easier. It's also a good idea to make a note of special feeding instructions, any medications the cat is taking, the name and phone number of your veterinarian, and where you can be reached in an emergency.

# 15
# The Cat Show

The purchaser of a pedigreed cat or kitten sooner or later toys with the idea of exhibiting his treasure in the show-ring. It is largely a matter of pride of possession. The owner wants to prove that his cat is as beautiful as any other, and that maybe he can even win a ribbon or two.

There are many advantages to exhibiting cats, not the least of which is meeting other people who are interested in cats and their welfare. Certain of a sympathetic ear, the newcomer at the show can discuss with acquaintances his problems in raising and training. He learns a lot he never knew before. In short, his friend the cat has opened up an entirely new interest, and almost before he is aware of it, he has become a fancier as well as a pet owner. However, transformation from pet owner to fancier does not come about in a moment: It takes time. But a trip to a cat show will certainly speed things along.

The best way to learn what goes on at a cat show is to attend one first as a spectator. Your attention can then be given to observing the whole procedure: the preparation and handling of the cats, the judging rings and procedures, the general layout of the show, the concessionaires who sell cat supplies, and even the spectators. You will learn what is expected of you, and how to conduct yourself if you decide to enter your cat for competition.

The proceedings at a cat show may be confusing at first, so here's a brief explanation of what to expect. As soon as you arrive at the exhibition hall, you will see several rows of cages where the cats entered for competition are benched, or where they spend their time when they are not being judged. Many of these cages are decorated with colorful drapes, carpeting, cushions or beds, and each is fitted with a separate litter box.

Each cat entered in the show has been assigned a "benching" number, which is used in all cases to refer to that cat at the show. That same number is also listed in the catalog, along with the cat's name and its breeding particulars. When the judging in a particular ring is about to begin, an announcer calls out the numbers of competitors scheduled for that particular class. The announcer will say, for instance, "Burmese cats, numbers 110 to 119, to ring five."

As the numbers are called, the owners or handlers transfer their cats to cages in the judging area, which is called a "ring." They place their cats in the properly numbered cages, then step back and keep out of the way. They may not talk with the judge.

Inside the ring, each judge has a long table, overhung with spotlights, ready for his work. And in front of the table are rows of chairs to accommodate the spectators.

## HOW CATS ARE JUDGED

Purebred cats are judged individually against a written standard for their particular breed that describes the ideal specimen. The standard is composed of sections that define every part of the cat's conformation—head, skull, nose, muzzle, chin, jaw, ears, eyes, neck, body, legs, and tail—plus the type of coat and acceptable coat colors. Each section is assigned a point value, the combined total being one hundred.

After removing a cat from his cage, the judge brings him to the table for a hand examination. Holding him up expertly at eye level, he looks closely at the face, the mouth, the ears, and the eyes. Nothing escapes the judge's minute inspection. But he is not finished yet. Next, he places the cat on the table where he sets him up to study body make and shape, all the while keeping the animal under perfect control with a firm hand on the top of his back. It is clearly evident to the new show-goer that it takes a lot of expertise to judge a cat in this manner and have the cat right there when you get through!

The judge will examine all the cats in a particular class, looking for those that in his opinion most closely conform to the breed standard. A group of seven or eight black Persians may look alike to many spectators, for instance, but the seasoned judge will quickly notice the subtle distinctions that determine the order in which he will place the cats. The judge then makes a decision and places the ribbons on the cages behind him.

The cats not being judged at the moment are comfortably snoozing in their cages in the benching area, usually with their backs to the aisle as a sort of wordless *do not disturb* sign. Or perhaps they are being held in their owners' arms, stroked and talked to if they happen to be a bit nervous. In fact, few if any cages are left without someone in charge to see that the cat is given every care.

## BREAKING INTO THE SHOW WORLD

Situated in various sections of the country are innumerable clubs composed of fanciers banded together for the advancement of pedigreed cats. They select and mate their stock carefully; they produce sparingly. They aim for health, beauty, and good temperament as well as for uniformity in accordance with the standard characteristics for each breed as prescribed by the registration agency with which their club is affiliated as a member.

There are several cat registries, the largest and most influential being the Cat Fanciers' Association, Inc., with about six hundred member clubs in the United States, Canada, and Japan. A nonprofit organization that registers cats and kittens, CFA has published studbooks for the past seventy years or more and has registered hundreds of thousands of cats as well as more than twenty thousand individual cattery names. CFA formulates rules for the management of cat shows and seeks to promote the interests of breeders and exhibitors, and to improve the various breeds of cats. Headquarters are presently located at 1309 Allaire Avenue, Ocean, New Jersey 07712.

## TYPES OF SHOWS

There are several different show formats that cat clubs use. Unless you are aware of them, you may arrive at the show site and learn that your cat isn't scheduled until the next day, or worse yet, that it should have been shown the day before.

Cat shows are usually held on weekends and may be one- or two-day affairs. They can be "allbreed" or "split" formats. An allbreed event usually means that all the different breeds will be present for the duration of the show. In a split format, all shorthairs might be scheduled on one day and all longhairs the next, with Household Pets being judged on one predetermined day. Or perhaps all Championship classes will be judged one day, and all Kittens, Premiership, and Household Pets the next.

Depending on the chosen format, each cat entered in a show is judged several times. The lines that follow a cat's name and number in the show catalog indicate how many times he will be judged during the course of the show.

## HOW TO ENTER A SHOW

To learn about forthcoming shows in your area, contact your local cat club or consult the "Show Calendar" section of *Cat Fancy* magazine or the "To Show and Go" column of *Cats* magazine. Both periodicals (usually available at newsstands) list upcoming shows throughout the country by date, state, city, and location. The name, address, and phone number of the show's Entry Clerk will also appear. At least eight weeks before the show date, write to the Entry Clerk and request an information flyer plus an entry form for each cat you plan to exhibit. Don't hesitate to mention that you are a new exhibitor; many clubs make helpful pamphlets available to newcomers.

The show flyer will specify (along with the date and location) the show hours, the judges for each breed, the classes that may be entered, the cost of entries, cage fees, all other show regulations, the entry closing date, and the name and address of the person to whom entries should be sent.

## COMPLETING THE ENTRY BLANK:
## SHOW CLASSES

Read the entry form carefully before you fill it out, for even the slightest error could cause your cat to be disqualified. Enter your cat's name, registration number, birthdate, sex, eye color, breed, color, the names of his sire and dam, plus your name, address, and telephone number. Much of this information appears on your registration certificate and should be copied exactly.

The bottom of the entry form will contain a space for you to indicate the class in which you are entering your cat. Cats can compete in four major categories at shows: *Non-Championship* and *Championship* classes for registered cats of recognized breeds that have not been spayed or castrated, *Premiership* classes for spayed and castrated registered purebred cats, and *Household Pets*. Cats that have not been spayed or castrated compete for Championships and Grand Championships, while the altered cats compete for Premier and Grand Premier titles.

The following is a short description of the *Non-Championship* classes of the CFA:

*Kitten:* For kittens over four months of age and under eight months on the opening day of the show.

*Household Pet:* For domestic kittens or cats of unknown ancestry or unregistered lineage. Cats over eight months old must be neutered or spayed to be eligible to be shown. Kittens need not be altered. Household Pets can be any size or color, but they must not be declawed. Since Household Pets have no standard of points against which they are evaluated, they are judged on condition, grooming, beauty, coloring, and temperament when handled.

*Provisional Breed:* For pedigreed cats or kittens of a breed that has a standard provisionally accepted by CFA but is not yet recognized for championship competition.

The following is a short description of the *Championship* classes:

*Open Class:* For registered cats eight months of age or older on the first day of the show that have not yet completed requirements for championship competition.

*Champion Class:* For cats that are recognized Champions according to the association's rules but are not yet confirmed Grand Champions.

*Grand Champion Class:* For cats that have earned by wins and points the title of Grand Champion according to the rules of the association. In CFA, for example, cats (while champions) that have beaten two hundred other Champions, either in breed or by making final wins, are eligible.

The following is a short description of the *Premiership* classes:

*Open Class:* For neutered and spayed cats over eight months of age that have not yet completed a Premiership.

*Premier:* For neutered and spayed cats that are recognized Premiers according to the association's rules but that have not yet completed Grand Premierships.

*Grand Premier:* For neutered and spayed cats that have earned by wins and points the title of Grand Premier according to the rules of the association. In the CFA, for instance, this includes cats (while Premiers) that have beaten seventy-five other Premiers by placing above them in the finals.

In addition to the registration information, you will also notice space on the entry form to indicate your cage requirements, such as "double cage" or "sales cage." The latter is not a cage you can buy, but one you can rent for kittens you want to sell. Glance over the form to be sure all details are correct, then sign and date your entry. Mail it, along with a check for the entry fees, to the clerk before the closing date.

Within a few weeks, you will receive a confirmation of its receipt from the Entry Clerk. This will list your cat's name, breed, and the classes in which he is entered, along with his identification number for the day. This will be your cat's benching number as well as his identification number in the catalog. If there are any errors, call the Clerk immediately so they can be corrected before the catalog is printed.

## PREPARING YOUR CAT FOR THE SHOW

Once your entry has been accepted, the next step is to start getting your cat ready. If your cat is not used to being caged, begin confining him for a few minutes each day, gradually increasing the time. Get him accustomed to being handled and stroked, too. Cats that are not used to being caged or handled often become hostile; you could be disqualified from showing if your cat bites a judge.

Cats that are shown should be sparkling clean and free of dead hair; those with long hair should be free of mats and tangles. Start a daily grooming routine at least a month before the show. Chapter 9 describes grooming techniques for both shorthairs and longhairs.

Clip the claws on all four feet, if necessary, a day or two before the show so that no one will be scratched. Be sure to check the ears, too. Clean away any dirt or excess wax with a cotton ball moistened with warm water. To be admitted to the show, your cat's vaccinations must be current, and the cat himself should be free of mites, fungus, and signs of infectious or contagious disease.

## SUPPLIES FOR THE SHOW

The cage provided for your cat at the show is made of heavy-gauge wire with a galvanized metal pan on the bottom. Many cat clubs ask exhibitors to cover two or three sides of the cage. Without some kind of drape, neighboring cats might hiss at each other all day and cause normally placid animals to become ruffled. You should select washable material (in a color that enhances the appearance of your cat) and make drapes for the cage. The entry form often indicates the size of the show cages being used. Most show cages are fairly uniform in size: a single cage usually measures about 24 by 24 by 24 inches, and a double cage about 24 by 24 by 48 inches. Safety pins or clothespins will keep the drapes in place. Don't forget a covering for the cage floor—a towel or a fluffy bath mat will keep your cat comfortable and be easy to clean in the event of an accident. Although it's not necessary to go overboard with decorations, some clubs present awards for the best decorated cages.

Most of your cat's grooming will be done at home before the show, but you'll need to take along certain supplies for last minute touch-ups. Depending on your cat's coat type, pack comb(s), brush, nail trimmer, grooming powder, an antistatic coat dressing, cotton swabs, and a clean chamois or silk scarf. If your cat has long hair, take along a small grooming table. Don't forget a roll of paper towels and a *nontoxic* disinfectant, too. Although the cages provided are clean, many exhibitors like to sanitize the cages before putting their cats inside.

The show management usually provides disposable litter boxes, litter, and cardboard food and water dishes, although you may want to take along your own to make your cat feel at home. Most shows make cat food available to exhibitors, but if you are traveling long distances, it's a good idea to take along your cat's regular food and a supply of your own water to avoid digestive upsets.

### THE BIG DAY

On the day of the show, plan to arrive at the show site early so that you can unload your equipment, check in, set up your cage, locate the judging rings, and put the finishing touches on your cat in a relaxed manner. Your cat should travel to the show in a sturdy carrier, clearly labeled with your name and address.

When you enter the show hall, someone will check in your cat, give you your benching slip, and direct you to the proper row of cages. The front of the cage assigned to you will bear the identification number assigned when your cat's entry was confirmed. Remember it. Your cat will be listed under this number in the catalog and will be called to the judging ring by this number. Identification numbers are used at both cat and dog shows so judges do not know the identities of the entries.

Disinfect the cage before you hang the drapes and organize the inside. Take your cat out of his carrier and place him in the benching cage. A few favorite toys will have a comforting effect.

Consult the judging schedule to learn when your cat will be judged. Allow ample time to get your cat ready. During the course of the show, you will hear numbers being called over the loudspeaker system. It is an exhibitor's responsibility to check the progress in the judging rings and to pay attention to the numbers being called. As soon as you hear your number, take your cat promptly to the ring and put him inside the cage marked with your identification number.

# 16
# The Cat Breeds

In this chapter, you will meet thirty purebred cats. Twenty-seven breeds are officially recognized for registration and championship competition by the Cat Fanciers' Association, Inc. (CFA), the largest registry in the world. The three remaining breeds have been granted provisional status by the CFA. This means that although judges have the opportunity to evaluate a breed according to a provisional standard, the breed is not yet accepted for championship competition. Provisional status, however, usually is the last important step before a breed is advanced to championship status in an association.

The following short descriptions detail the origins of each breed, highlight a few personality traits, and suggest the grooming requirements. Also included are the fine points of each breed's conformation and a list of accepted coat colors and markings adapted from the show standards of the CFA.

Every breed eligible for registration with a cat fanciers' organization has an official standard or written description that depicts the ideal feline of that breed. In general terms, the standard describes every part of the cat's conformation: the structure and contour of the head;

the shape, size, color, and placement of the eyes; the outline and carriage of the ears; the size and shape of the body; the length and proportions of the legs; the shape of the paws and the number of toes; the length and thickness of the tail, as well as the type and color of the coat. Put the various parts together and you have a word picture of the perfect specimen.

No written standard, however, can describe a breed precisely. Each living and breathing cat is an individual and should be evaluated as such. A standard describes the ultimate example of a breed—a sum total that is virtually impossible to attain in any living specimen. Essentially, standards are guidelines by which judges can evaluate cats at shows and by which breeders can assess their progress toward producing the ideal feline.

At the end of this chapter you will also find some information about rare breeds, plus a few additional breeds that are recognized by registries other than the CFA.

If you own a non-pedigreed cat, don't be too disappointed that the apple of your eye isn't included. Randomly bred cats constitute the majority of domestic cats throughout the world. More than forty million of them live in the United States today. Non-pedigreed cats come in a variety of shapes, sizes, coat colors, and markings, and they all have one delightful attribute in common—uniqueness. And even though their parentage over the past few generations has not been tightly controlled, many of them do look very much like certain pedigreed breeds.

## *Abyssinian*

- Very intelligent; trainable
- Extremely affectionate
- Active and playful; people-oriented
- Good-natured with children and other pets
- Soft, melodious voice
- Shorthaired; easy to groom

Although there is some disagreement about their ancestry, Abyssinians probably originated in Ethiopia (formerly Abyssinia) or Egypt long before the birth of Christ. More than any other modern breed, they closely resemble the sacred cats depicted in ancient Egyptian carvings and paintings. They were first brought to the United States around 1909.

The Abyssinian is a medium-sized, regal-looking cat with a lithe and graceful body, and proportionately slim, fine-boned legs and feet. The head is a slightly rounded wedge shape. The forehead is wide and the almond-shaped eyes are gold or green. The ears are large and broad at the base with pointed tips. The tail is fairly long and tapering. The soft, silky, resilient coat has been compared with that of the English wild hare, from which the breed gets its nickname, "bunny cat." Each hair is ticked with two or three bands of darker color.

COLORS: Ruddy, Red, and Blue.

*American Shorthair*

- Intelligent
- Healthy and hardy
- Loving and sociable
- Wonderful housepet; friendly with children and other pets

- Reasonably quiet
- Shorthaired; easy to groom

The American Shorthair's ancestors were brought to North America in the seventeenth century by early settlers. They controlled the rat population during the voyages of the *Mayflower* and other early ships, as well as in the Colonies.

This is a very athletic cat with a medium to large, powerful body; well-developed chest; heavy shoulders; strong and heavily muscled legs; and firm, rounded paws. The head is large with full cheeks, square muzzle, and well-developed chin. The round and wide eyes are slightly slanting, and the ears are slightly rounded at the tips. The short, thick coat is hard in texture.

COLORS: White, Black, Blue, Red, Cream, Chinchilla, Shaded Silver, Shell Cameo (Red Chinchilla), Shaded Cameo (Red Shaded), Black Smoke, Blue Smoke, Cameo Smoke (Red Smoke), Tortoiseshell Smoke, Classic Tabby Pattern, Mackerel Tabby Pattern, Patched Tabby Pattern, Brown Patched Tabby, Blue Patched Tabby, Silver Patched Tabby, Silver Tabby, Red Tabby, Brown Tabby, Blue Tabby, Cream Tabby, Cameo Tabby, Tortoiseshell, Calico, Dilute Calico, Blue-Cream, Bi-Color, Van Bi-Color, Van Calico, and Van Blue-Cream and White.

### *American Wirehair*

- Intelligent
- Affectionate and good-natured
- Healthy and sturdy
- Moderately quiet
- Friendly with children and other pets
- Medium-length crimped coat; easy to groom

The first American Wirehair, a red and white male, appeared in 1966 as a spontaneous mutation in a litter of shorthaired farm cats.

American Wirehairs resemble American Shorthairs in conformation: medium to large body with well-rounded torso; medium-length, well-muscled legs; oval and compact paws; tapering tail; round head with prominent cheekbones; large, round eyes, and a firm, well-developed chin. The conspicuous difference is the Wirehair's springy, coarse, and resilient coat. The individual hairs are crimped or bent—even the hair within the ears. The whiskers are also crimped or curly.

COLORS: White, Black, Blue, Red, Cream, Chinchilla, Shaded Silver, Shell Cameo (Red Chinchilla), Shaded Cameo (Red Shaded), Black Smoke, Blue Smoke, Cameo Smoke (Red Smoke), Classic Tabby Pattern, Mackerel Tabby Pattern, Silver Tabby, Red Tabby, Brown Tabby, Blue Tabby, Cream Tabby, Cameo Tabby, Tortoiseshell, Calico, Dilute Calico, Blue-Cream, Bi-Color, and OWC (Other Wirehair Colors)—any other color or pattern with the exception of those showing evidence of hybridization resulting in the colors chocolate, lavender, the Himalayan pattern, or these combinations with white.

### *Balinese*

- Very intelligent; trainable
- Affectionate and good-natured
- Playful; likes human companionship
- Friendly with children
- Somewhat vocal, but voice not as shrill as that of its relative, the Siamese
- Silky, fine long hair; needs regular grooming

The Balinese looks like the Siamese except that it has long and silky hair. The breed was developed in the United States from longhaired kittens that occasionally appeared in Siamese litters. Recognized as a breed in 1963, they were named because their fluid movements resemble those of Balinese dancers.

The Balinese is a dainty cat with a long and svelte body, long and slim legs, dainty and small paws, and a long and magnificently plumed tail. It has a long, tapering wedge head; long and straight nose; and fine, wedge-shaped muzzle. The ears are strikingly large and pointed, and the almond-shaped eyes are a deep vivid blue. The fine and silky coat is without downy undercoat, an even tone all over contrasting with the dense and clearly defined mask and points.

COLORS: Seal Point, Chocolate Point, Blue Point, and Lilac Point.

### Birman (Sacred Cat of Burma)

- Intelligent; easy to train
- High-spirited and playful
- Very affectionate; likes people

- Friendly with children
- Quiet voice
- Long, silky hair; needs daily grooming

Birmans are thought to have originated centuries ago in the temples of Burma. According to legend, they once were pure white with yellow eyes. One white cat, Sinh, was the favorite of a high priest named Mun-Ha. During a raid on the temple, Mun-Ha was attacked. As he lay dying, he was touched by Sinh. The priest's spirit entered the cat, which was suddenly transformed. His white coat turned to gold, and his eyes became sapphire blue. His face, tail, and legs became dark, but the paws that had touched the priest remained white as a symbol of purity.

Birmans are stocky, long-bodied cats with heavy, medium-length legs, large round paws, and bushy tails. Their heads are broad and round with full cheeks, and they have almost round, deep blue eyes. They have long, silky hair that forms a heavy ruff around the neck. The breed's most distinctive features are white gloves on all four paws. Those on the back feet extend partially up the back legs to end in points known as "laces."

COLORS: Seal Point, Blue Point, Chocolate Point, and Lilac Point.

### Bombay

- Intelligent; easy to train
- Likes attention and companionship
- Charming personality
- Good-natured with children and other pets
- Moderately quiet
- Shorthaired; easy to groom

The elegant, jet-black Bombay was developed by crossing sable brown Burmese with black American Shorthairs. The goal was to create a creature resembling the black panther that lives in India. The breeding program began in 1958, but it was not until 1976 that the CFA approved a standard for Bombays.

This is a well-balanced, medium-sized cat, similar in conformation to the Burmese, with a pleasingly round head with no sharp angles. The face is full, with considerable breadth between the eyes, tapering to a short muzzle. The huge eyes range from gold to deep copper in color. The broad-based ears with rounded tips tilt slightly forward. The close-lying, jet-black, satiny coat has a high, patent leather sheen.

COLOR: Black.

### British Shorthair

- Intelligent; devoted
- Strong and sturdy
- Placid and gentle; friendly with children and other pets

- Good mouser
- Quiet; soft voice
- Shorthaired; easy to groom

British Shorthairs were developed in the late nine-teenth century by selectively breeding choice street cats. Right after World War II, they were crossed with Persians to improve type. The breedings produced handsome cats with the sturdiness and hardiness of the shorthairs, and the broad head and large round eyes of the longhairs.

British Shorthairs are large, compact, and powerful cats with powerful bodies, strong, well-boned legs, round and firm paws, and thick tapering tails. They have round and massive heads with round cheeks, broad noses, well-developed chins, and short, thick necks. The medium-sized ears are broad at the base and rounded at the tips. The eyes are large and round. The coat is short, very dense, and resilient.

COLORS: White, Black, Blue, Cream, Black Smoke, Blue Smoke, Classic Tabby Pattern, Mackerel Tabby Pattern, Silver Tabby, Red Tabby, Brown Tabby, Blue Tabby, Cream Tabby, Spotted Tabby Pattern, Tortoiseshell, Calico, Blue-Cream, and Bi-Color.

### *Burmese*

- Very intelligent and easy to train
- Very social; loves people
- Extremely affectionate
- Friendly with children and other pets
- Somewhat vocal but not as chatty as the Siamese
- Shorthaired; easy to groom

Nearly all Burmese—as we know the breed today—descend from one brown, Oriental-type female named Wong Mau that was imported to the United States from Rangoon in 1930. Since no Burmese male was available, she was mated with a Siamese. All resulting kittens were hybrids. When the males were mated back to their mother, the first dark-coated Burmese were produced. The CFA recognized the Burmese in 1936.

This is a charming, "Teddy Bear" of a cat with a medium-sized, muscular body, an ample and rounded chest, and well-proportioned legs. The head is pleasingly round, with considerable breadth between the eyes, blending into a broad and well-developed short muzzle. The medium-sized ears are set well apart—broad at the base and rounded at the tips—and tilt slightly forward. Large, expressive eyes that range from yellow to gold enhance the Burmese's sweet expression. The short, glossy coat has a satiny texture.

COLORS: Sable, Champagne, Blue, and Platinum.

### *Chartreux*

- Intelligent; trainable
- Healthy and robust; famed for its hunting prowess
- Loving and devoted
- Good-natured with children and other pets
- Quiet; soft voice
- Medium-short fur; easy to groom

The handsome Chartreux is one of the oldest natural breeds. Its history dates back to sixteenth-century France, where it was bred by the Carthusian monks, who also produced the aromatic Chartreuse liqueur.

The Chartreux is similar in conformation and coloring to the blue British Shorthair. Its husky, robust physique, neither cobby (short-bodied), nor classic, is often termed "primitive." Females are medium-sized; males may grow twice as large. The head is round and broad but not a sphere, with full cheeks and powerful jaws. The large, round, expressive eyes range from copper to gold.

The medium-sized ears are very erect and set high on the head. The medium-short coat is dense and slightly woolly in texture. Chartreux are hardy creatures that are famed in French literature for being fearless watchcats and fantastic mousers. In France, they are called "doglike" cats. As of this writing, Chartreux have been granted CFA provisional status.

COLOR: Any shade of blue-gray from ash to slate, the tips lightly brushed with silver.

### *Colorpoint Shorthair*

- Very intelligent; easy to train
- Very sociable; adores companionship
- Very active; demanding
- Exotic-looking; gorgeous coloring
- Extremely talkative; distinctive voice
- Short, fine-textured coat; easy to groom

Colorpoint Shorthairs are essentially Siamese-type cats with points (mask, ears, feet, legs, and tail) other than seal, chocolate, blue, or lilac. The new colors were created by breeding Siamese to other varieties, particularly American Shorthairs.

Colorpoints are svelte, dainty cats with long tapering lines, very lithe but muscular. They resemble Siamese in conformation: long, tapering wedge-shaped head; fine wedge-shaped muzzle; vivid blue almond-shaped eyes; striking, large pointed ears; long and slender neck; long body; long and slim legs; dainty oval paws; long and thin tapering tail. The fine, glossy coat lies close to the body.

COLORS: Red Point, Cream Point, Seal-Lynx Point, Chocolate-Lynx Point, Blue-Lynx Point, Lilac-Lynx Point, Red-Lynx Point, Seal-Tortie Point, Chocolate-

Tortie Point, Blue-Cream Point, Lilac-Cream Point, Seal Tortie-Lynx Point, Chocolate Tortie-Lynx Point, Blue-Cream Lynx Point, Lilac-Cream Lynx Point, and Cream Lynx Point.

***Egyptian Mau***

- Intelligent
- Loving and devoted; people-oriented
- Very active and playful
- Good-natured with children and other pets
- Moderately vocal; soft and lyrical voice
- Short, fine-textured coat; easy to groom

The Egyptian Mau (*mau* is the Egyptian word for cat) is the only natural domesticated breed of spotted cat. It is said that their spots appear not only on their coat pattern but also on their skin. The Mau's ancestors can be traced back to 1400 B.C. in Egyptian art. Maus were first seen in Europe at a cat show in Rome during the early 1950s. From there they were brought to the United States by Princess Troubetsky.

The Egyptian Mau is a colorful, medium-sized cat with a long, graceful body and slightly tapering tail. Its hind legs are proportionately longer than its front legs, creating the appearance of being on tip-toe when the Mau is standing upright. The head is a slightly rounded wedge with large, almond-shaped, gooseberry-green eyes that slant toward the ears. The ears are large, wide apart, erect, and moderately pointed. The medium-length coat is silky and fine with a lustrous sheen.

COLORS: Silver, Bronze, and Smoke.

### *Exotic Shorthair*

- Intelligent
- Healthy and robust
- Extremely affectionate; sweet temperament
- Good-natured with children and other pets
- Quiet; soft voice
- Medium-length plush coat; needs regular grooming but not as much as most longhairs

Exotic Shorthairs were developed in the 1960s by crossing Persians with American Shorthairs. The object was to produce a Persian-type cat with short hair.

This striking cat resembles the Persian in conformation, with its deep-chested, compact body that is equally massive across the shoulders and rump, with a short and well-rounded middle piece. The head—round and massive, with a short, snub nose, full cheeks, broad and powerful jaws—is set on a short, thick neck. The round and full eyes may be brilliant copper, green, or blue-green in color. The ears are small, round tipped, and tilt forward.

The soft, plush coat is medium in length, slightly longer than other shorthairs but not long enough to flow. Like Persians, Exotics come in a dazzling array of coat colors and patterns.

COLORS: White, Black, Blue, Red, Cream, Chocolate, Lilac, Chinchilla, Shaded Silver, Chinchilla Golden, Shaded Golden, Shell Cameo (Red Chinchilla), Shaded Cameo (Red Shaded), Shell Tortoiseshell, Shaded Tortoiseshell, Black Smoke, Blue Smoke, Cameo Smoke (Red Smoke), Smoke Tortoiseshell, Blue-Cream Smoke, Classic Tabby Pattern, Mackerel Tabby Pattern, Patched Tabby Pattern, Brown Patched Tabby, Blue Patched Tabby, Silver Patched Tabby, Silver Tabby, Red Tabby, Brown Tabby, Blue Tabby, Cream Tabby, Cameo Tabby, Peke-Faced Red and Peke-Faced Red Tabby, Tortoiseshell, Calico, Dilute Calico, Blue-Cream, Bi-Color, Van Bi-Color, Van Calico, Van Blue-Cream and White, Tabby and White, Seal Point, Chocolate Point, Blue Point, Lilac Point, Flame (Red) Point, Cream Point, Tortie Point, Blue-Cream Point, Seal Lynx-Point, and Blue Lynx-Point.

### *Havana Brown*

- Intelligent; trainable
- Active; playful
- Charming companion; can become very attached to owner
- Good-natured with children and other pets
- Moderately talkative
- Shorthaired; easy to groom

A few solid mahogany brown cats were recorded in the late nineteenth century. It was only in the early 1950s, however, that a serious attempt was made to produce solid brown cats that would breed true. This was accomplished through crosses of Seal-Point Siamese with black domestic shorthairs. The breed was named because its deep, rich tobacco color resembled that of a Havana cigar. The color is altogether different in appearance from the sable brown of the Burmese cat.

The Havana Brown is a dramatic-looking, medium-sized cat with a firm, muscular body and slender, tapering tail. It stands relatively high on its legs. The head is slightly longer than it is wide, narrowing to a rounded muzzle with a break on each side behind the whisker pads. The oval-shaped eyes may be any vivid shade of green—the deeper the color, the better. Large, forward-tilting ears give the Havana an alert appearance. The smooth and lustrous coat is solid-colored to the roots; even the whiskers are brown.

COLOR: A rich, even shade of warm brown.

### *Himalayan*

- Intelligent
- Meticulous habits; fine apartment pet
- Devoted and affectionate
- Friendly with children and other pets
- Somewhat talkative, but with a soft voice
- Long and thick hair; requires a great deal of grooming

Himalayans were the result of selective breeding programs in which Persians and Siamese were crossbred. The goal was to produce cats that had the body type of Persians with the distinctive point coloring of the Siamese. The breed, identical in conformation to the Persian, was named because the coat pattern resembled that of the Himalayan rabbit. It was accepted as a breed in 1957. Breeding Himalayan to Himalayan through the years, however, began to result in inferior type and scanty coats. As of February 20, 1984, the Cat Fanciers'

Association reclassified the Himalayan as a color variety of the Persian.

The Himalayan has a compact, deep-chested body that is massive across the shoulders and rump, and short, thick legs. The head is round and massive, the nose short and snub, and the cheeks full. The brilliant round eyes are set far apart, giving a sweet expression to the face. The ears are small, round-tipped, and tilted forward. The coat is long and thick, standing off from the body, with an immense ruff that extends into a deep frill between the front legs.

COLORS: (These are also listed under the "Persian colors" entry)—Seal Point, Chocolate Point, Blue Point, Lilac Point, Flame (Red) Point, Cream Point, Tortie Point, Blue-Cream Point, Seal Lynx-Point, Blue Lynx-Point, Chocolate Solid Point, and Lilac Solid Color.

### *Japanese Bobtail*

- Intelligent
- Very loving and devoted
- Charming disposition
- Friendly with children and other pets
- Somewhat talkative; delicate voice
- Medium-length coat; easy to groom

Japanese Bobtails have existed for centuries in Japan. In their traditional tri-colored coat of black, red, and white, known as Mi-Ke (pronounced mee-kay), they were thought to bring good fortune to their owners.

This is a medium-sized cat with clean lines and bone

structure—well muscled, but straight and slender rather than massive in build. The head forms an almost perfect equilateral triangle with gentle curving lines. The unique set of the large eyes, combined with high cheekbones and a long parallel nose, lends a distinctive Japanese cast to the Bobtail's face, especially in profile, which is completely different from the other Oriental breeds. The breed's most distinctive feature is its short tail with hair that fans out in a sort of pompon resembling that of a bunny. The soft, silky coat is almost nonshedding.

COLORS: White, Black, Red, Black and White, Red and White, Mi-Ke (Tri-Color), Tortoiseshell, and OJBC (Other Japanese Bobtail Colors)—including the following categories and any color, pattern, or combination thereof except coloring that is point-restricted (i.e., Siamese markings) or unpatterned agouti (i.e., Abyssinian coloring): "Patterned" categories denote and include any variety of tabby striping or spotting with or without areas of solid (unmarked) color, with preference given to bold, dramatic markings and rich, vivid coloring. Other Solid Colors: Blue or Cream. Patterned Self-Colors: Red, black, blue, cream, silver, or brown. Other Bi-Colors: Blue and white or cream and white. Patterned Bi-Colors: Red, black, blue, cream, silver, or brown combined with white. Patterned Tortoiseshell: Blue-Cream. Patterned Blue-Cream. Dilute Tri-Colors: Blue, cream, and white. Patterned Dilute Tri-Colors: Patterned Mi-Ke (Tri-Color), and Tortoiseshell with white.

## *Javanese*

- Very intelligent; trainable
- Affectionate and good-natured
- Playful; likes human companionship
- Friendly with children

- Somewhat vocal, but not as shrill as its relative, the Siamese
- Silky, fine long hair; needs regular grooming

The Javanese looks like the Siamese except that it has long and silky hair. Like the Balinese, the Javanese was developed from Siamese parents with a mutant gene for long hair. Actually, CFA recognizes the Seal Point, Chocolate Point, Blue Point, and Lilac Point "longhaired Siamese" as Balinese, while those of other colors are known as Javanese.

The Javanese bears the same breed standard as the Balinese. It is a dainty cat with a long and svelte body, long and slim legs, and a long, plumed tail. The head is a long, tapering wedge that starts at the nose and flares out in straight lines to the tips of the ears to form a triangle with no break at the whiskers. The strikingly large ears are pointed, and the almond-shaped eyes are a deep, vivid blue.

COLORS: Red Point, Cream Point, Seal-Lynx Point, Chocolate-Lynx Point, Blue-Lynx Point, Lilac-Lynx Point, Red-Lynx Point, Chocolate Tortie-Lynx Point, Blue-Cream Lynx Point, Lilac-Cream Lynx Point, Cream Lynx Point, Seal Tortie-Lynx Point, Seal-Tortie Point, Chocolate-Tortie Point, Blue-Cream Point, and Lilac-Cream Point.

### *Korat*

- Intelligent; trainable
- Affectionate and devoted
- Often becomes attached to one person
- Friendly with thoughtful children and good-natured pets

- Quiet; likes peaceful atmosphere and gentle people
- Short to medium fur; easy to groom

An ancient natural breed, this silvery blue cat is from the Korat Plateau in Thailand (formerly Siam). In its native land it is also known as the Si-Sawat ("si" stands for color and "sawat" is a wild blue fruit). For centuries Korats have been highly prized and considered symbols of good luck by the Thai people. They were never sold but given as gifts on special occasions.

The Korat is a medium-sized cat with a muscular, supple body and a feeling of hard-coiled "spring" power and unexpected weight. The males, renowned in Thailand for their prowess as fighters, should look the part—powerful and fit—while females should be smaller and daintier. The head is heart-shaped with a strong and well-developed chin and jaw. The large and luminous green eyes, oversized for the face, are particularly prominent with an extraordinary depth and brilliance. The ears are large, with rounded tips, and are set high on the head. The glossy and fine silver blue coat is tipped with silver, giving the Korat an elegant, shimmering look.

COLOR: Silver blue, tipped with silver.

## Maine Coon

- Intelligent; excellent mouser
- Healthy and robust; matures slowly
- Energetic; playful
- Gentle and devoted; friendly with children
- Fairly quiet; makes gentle chirping sounds
- Heavy, shaggy coat; needs frequent grooming

The Maine Coon's ancestry traces back to the cats brought to New England by sailors and early settlers. The breed probably developed through crosses of Angoras with various domestic shorthairs.

The Maine Coon is a solid, rugged, medium- to large-sized cat. Its broad-chested body is long and muscular with all parts in proportion to create a rectangular appearance. The legs are substantial and wide set; the snowshoelike paws are large, round, and well tufted. The head is medium in width and medium-long in length with a squareness to the muzzle. The large and well-tufted ears are wide at the base and taper to a point. The eyes are large and wide set. The bushy tail is long and tapering. The silky-textured coat is heavy and shaggy, shorter on the shoulders, longer on the stomach and on the britches.

COLORS: Solid Color Class: White, Black, Blue, Red, and Cream. Tabby Color Class: Classic Tabby Pattern, Mackerel Tabby Pattern, Silver Tabby, Red Tabby, Brown Tabby, Blue Tabby, Cream Tabby, Cameo Tabby, and Patched Tabby Pattern. Tabby with White Class: Tabby with White, Patched Tabby with White. Parti-Color Class: Tortoiseshell, Tortoiseshell with White, Calico, Dilute Calico, Blue-Cream, Blue-Cream with White, and Bi-Color. Other Maine Coon Colors Class: Chinchilla, Shaded Silver, Shell Cameo, Shaded Cameo (Red Shaded), Black Smoke, Blue Smoke, and Cameo Smoke (Red Smoke).

## *Manx*

- Tailless; unique appearance
- Intelligent; excellent mouser
- Loving and devoted; matures slowly
- Playful; friendly with children
- Somewhat talkative
- Shorthaired; easy to groom

Although tailless cats have been known for centuries in many parts of the world, the Manx is closely associated with the Isle of Man. They were possibly brought to this remote island on Oriental trading ships. Kittens with three different tail lengths—"rumpy" (completely tailless), "stumpy" (very short tail), and "taily" (complete tail)—can be produced in the same litter. Only the tailless Manx is eligible for show.

The Manx is a powerful-looking, compact cat that presents an overall impression of roundness: a round head with firm, round muzzle, prominent cheeks, and a jowly appearance; large, round eyes set at a slight angle toward the nose; broad chest and well-sprung ribs; heavily boned short front legs; short back that arches from the shoulders to a round rump; longer hind legs that make the rump considerably higher than the shoulders; great depth of flank; rounded, muscular thighs; and large, round paws. The short and plush double-coat is cottony underneath and glossy on top.

COLORS: White, Black, Blue, Red, Cream, Chinchilla, Shaded Silver, Black Smoke, Blue Smoke, Classic Tabby Pattern, Mackerel Tabby Pattern, Patched Tabby Pattern, Brown Patched Tabby, Blue Patched Tabby, Silver Patched Tabby, Silver Tabby, Red Tabby, Brown Tabby, Blue Tabby, Cream Tabby, Tortoiseshell, Calico, Dilute Calico, Blue-Cream, Bi-Color, and OMC (Other Manx Colors)—any color or pattern with the exception of those showing hybridization resulting in the colors chocolate, lavender, the Himalayan pattern, or these combinations with white.

### *Ocicat*

- Intelligent; trainable
- Noted for its "wild" appearance
- Athletic, yet graceful and lithe
- People-oriented
- Friendly with children
- Short, sleek coat; easy to groom

The Ocicat was developed in the United States by crossing a Chocolate-Point Siamese male with a part-Abyssinian, part-Siamese female. The breed was named Ocicat because the first kitten, "Tonga," looked like a baby ocelot. The Ocicat has recently been granted CFA provisional status.

Ocicats are fairly large, exotic-looking, spotted cats. They are very athletic-looking animals with well-muscled, rather long bodies, with substantial bone and muscle development, and with powerful legs; yet they are lithe and graceful. The head is a modified wedge, with a well-defined muzzle, strong chin, and firm jaw. The large, almond-shaped eyes angle slightly upward toward the tufted ears. Ocicats have sleek, lustrous fur, patterned with spots and stripes, very similar to Egyptian Maus. They come in many colors with darker marks appearing on a lighter background.

COLORS: Tawny (Brown Spotted Tabby), Chocolate, Cinnamon, Blue, Lavender, Fawn, Silver, Chocolate Silver, Cinnamon Silver, Blue Silver, Lavender Silver, and Fawn Silver.

## Oriental Shorthair

- Very intelligent; trainable
- Agile; daring; acrobatic talents
- Likes attention; somewhat demanding
- Friendly with children and other pets
- Very talkative
- Shorthaired; easy to groom

Oriental Shorthairs are lithe and sleek Oriental-type cats with solid-colored, parti-colored, or patterned coats. They were produced by selective crosses of Siamese (for type) with other shorthairs (for color).

Oriental Shorthairs are similar to Siamese in conformation: long and svelte tubular body; long and slim legs (hind legs higher than those in front); dainty, oval paws; long, thin, tapering tail; long, tapering, wedge-shaped head; long, straight nose; almond-shaped eyes; strikingly large, pointed ears; and a long and slender neck. The coat is short and glossy, lying close to the body.

COLORS: Solid Colors Class: Blue, Chestnut, Cinnamon, Cream, Ebony, Fawn, Lavender, Red, and White. Shaded Colors Class: Blue-Cream Silver, Blue Silver, Cameo, Chestnut Silver, Chestnut-Tortie Silver, Cinnamon Silver, Cinnamon-Tortie Silver, Ebony Silver, Fawn Silver, Lavender-Cream Silver, Lavender Silver, and Tortoiseshell Silver. Smoke Colors Class: Blue Smoke, Cameo Smoke (Red Smoke), Chestnut Smoke, Cinnamon Smoke, Ebony Smoke, Fawn Smoke, Lavender Smoke, and Parti-Color Smoke. Tabby Colors Class: Classic Tabby Pattern, Mackerel Tabby Pattern, Patched Tabby Pattern, Spotted Tabby Pattern, Ticked Tabby Pattern, Blue Silver Tabby, Blue Tabby, Cameo Tabby, Cinnamon Silver Tabby, Cinnamon Tabby, Chestnut Silver Tabby, Chestnut Tabby, Cream Tabby, Ebony Tabby, Fawn Tabby, Lavender Silver Tabby, Lavender Tabby, Red Tabby, and Silver Tabby. Parti-Colors Color Class: Blue-Cream, Cinnamon Tortoiseshell, Chestnut-Tortie, Fawn-Cream, Lavender-Cream, and Tortoiseshell.

## *Persian*

- Stunning looking
- Peaceful; undemanding; bright
- Majestic; loves to be pampered
- Excellent apartment pet; meticulous habits
- Quiet; dainty voice
- Long and thick coat; needs frequent grooming

Longhaired cats were first known in Europe in the late sixteenth century. Although their ancestry is obscure, today's Persians mainly descend from the longhairs from Persia and the Angoras from Turkey that were brought to England in the late nineteenth century. As of February 1984, the Cat Fanciers' Association reclassified the Himalayan cat as a color variety of the Persian.

The Persian is a spectacular-looking, medium to large cat with a compact, deep-chested body that is massive across the shoulders and rump. Its legs are short and thick; the paws are large and round. The tail is short and very full. The Persian's round and massive head, round face, full cheeks, snub nose, broad and powerful jaws, and short, thick neck accentuate its massive appearance.

The finely textured coat is long and thick, and stands out from the body. It should be long all over. The ruff should be immense and should continue in a deep frill between the front legs. The tufts on the ears and between the toes should also be long. Persians come in over fifty color and coat patterns.

COLORS: White, Black, Blue, Red, Cream, Chocolate, Lilac, Chinchilla, Shaded Silver, Chinchilla Golden, Shaded Golden, Shell Cameo (Red Chinchilla), Shaded Cameo (Red Shaded), Shell Tortoiseshell, Shaded Tortoiseshell, Black Smoke, Blue Smoke, Cameo Smoke (Red Smoke), Smoke Tortoiseshell, Blue-Cream Smoke, Classic Tabby Pattern, Mackerel Tabby Pattern, Patched Tabby Pattern, Brown Patched Tabby, Blue Patched Tabby, Silver Patched Tabby, Silver Tabby, Red Tabby, Brown Tabby, Blue Tabby, Cream Tabby, Cameo Tabby, Tortoiseshell, Calico, Dilute Calico, Blue-Cream, Bi-Color, Persian Van Bi-Color, Persian Van Calico, Persian Van Dilute Calico, Tabby and White, Peke-Faced Red and Peke-Faced Red Tabby, Seal Point, Chocolate Point, Blue Point, Lilac Point, Flame (Red) Point, Cream Point, Tortie Point, Blue-Cream Point, Seal Lynx-Point, and Blue Lynx-Point.

## *Rexes: Cornish Rex and Devon Rex*

- Very intelligent; trainable
- Extremely affectionate and devoted
- Playful; inquisitive
- People-oriented; adores attention
- Reasonably quiet
- Short, curly, or wavy hair; marginal shedding; easy to groom

There are two distinct Rex breeds: the Cornish Rex and the Devon Rex. In 1950, a curly-coated red and white male named Kallibunker appeared in a normal litter of farm kittens in Cornwall, England. When mated back to his mother, more curly-coated kittens appeared in the litter. They were named after the curly-coated Rex rabbit.

Ten years later in nearby Devon, a wavy-coated kitten was born to a normal-coated female. He was assumed to be a Cornish Rex, but when mated to several of Kallibunker's progeny, all the offspring had straight coats. Geneticists soon determined that two Rex genes, Cornish (Gene I) and Devon (Gene II), existed that were different and incompatible.

Both Rex cats are fairly similar in conformation—with slender torsos; long, slim legs; small, oval paws; and long, whiplike tails. Their heads are different. The Cornish has a comparatively small and narrow head with a definite whisker break and a Roman nose; medium-to-large oval eyes that slant slightly upward; and large, erect, high-set ears. The Devon's head is a modified wedge with pronounced cheekbones, a nosebreak, and a whisker break. The Devon has large, wide-set eyes and large, low-set ears.

The most distinctive feature of each Rex cat is its short, curly fur, completely free of guard hairs. The Cor-

nish's coat lies close to the body like a tight, uniform mar-
cel wave, while the Devon's hair is softer, wavier, and
thinner. Both breeds even have wavy whiskers and eyebrows. Devon Rex cats come in over seventy-five color
and coat patterns, a spectrum that exceeds all other
breeds.

CORNISH REX COLORS: White, Black, Blue, Red, Cream,
Chinchilla, Shaded Silver, Black Smoke, Blue Smoke,
Classic Tabby Pattern, Mackerel Tabby Pattern, Patched
Tabby Pattern, Brown Patched Tabby, Blue Patched
Tabby, Silver Patched Tabby, Silver Tabby, Red Tabby,
Brown Tabby, Blue Tabby, Cream Tabby, Tortoiseshell,
Calico, Van Calico, Dilute Calico, Blue-Cream, Van
Blue-Cream and White, Bi-Color, Van Bi-Colors, and
ORC (Other Rex Colors)—any other color or pattern.

DEVON REX COLORS: White, Black, Blue, Red, Cream,
Chocolate, Lavender, Cinnamon, Fawn, Shaded Pattern,
Shaded Silver, Blue Shaded, Chocolate Shaded, Laven-
der Shaded, Cameo Shaded, Cinnamon Shaded, Fawn
Shaded, Tortoiseshell Shaded, Blue-Cream Shaded,
Chocolate Tortoiseshell Shaded, Cinnamon Tortoiseshell
Shaded, Lavender-Cream Shaded, Fawn-Cream
Shaded, Chinchilla, Smoke Pattern, Black Smoke, Blue
Smoke, Red Smoke Cameo (Cameo), Chocolate Smoke,
Lavender Smoke, Cinnamon Smoke, Cream Smoke,
Fawn Smoke, Tortoiseshell Smoke, Blue-Cream Smoke,
Chocolate Tortoiseshell Smoke, Lavender-Cream Smoke,
Cinnamon Tortoiseshell Smoke, Fawn-Cream Smoke,
Classic Tabby Pattern, Mackerel Tabby Pattern, Spotted
Tabby Pattern, Patched Tabby Pattern, Silver Tabby,
Brown Tabby, Blue Tabby, Red Tabby, Cream Tabby,
Chocolate (Chestnut), Chocolate Silver Tabby, Cinna-
mon Tabby, Cinnamon Silver Tabby, Lavender Tabby,
Lavender Silver Tabby, Fawn Tabby, Cameo Tabby, Blue

Silver, Cream Silver, and Fawn Silver Tabbies, Tortoise-shell, Blue-Cream, Chocolate (Chestnut) Tortoiseshell, Cinnamon Tortoiseshell, Lavender-Cream, Fawn-Cream, Calico, Van Calico, Dilute Calico, Dilute Van Calico, Bi-Color, Van Bi-Color, Fawn-Cream Calico, Lavender-Cream Calico, Cinnamon Cream Calico, and ODRC (Other Devon Rex Colors)—any other color or pattern.

### *Russian Blue*

- Intelligent; trainable
- Mild-tempered; likes peaceful surroundings
- Excellent apartment pet
- Loving and devoted
- Quiet; gentle voice
- Plush short hair; easy to groom

The Russian Blue is thought to have descended from blue cats with beaverlike coats that once lived in northern Russia. Experts believe the breed was brought to England in the 1860s by sailors from the Russian seaport of Archangel. In fact, the Russian Blue was once known as the Archangel cat.

This is a graceful and lithe cat with a firm, muscular

body; long and fine-boned legs; and a long, tapering tail. The top of the head is flat and long; the face is broad across the eyes. The vivid green eyes are round in shape and set wide apart. The ears are rather large and wide at the base, with tips that are more pointed than rounded; they are set far apart, as much on the side as on the top of the head. The bright blue coat is one of the hallmarks of the breed. It is dense and plush, like sealskin, with silver-tipped guard hairs that add a lustrous sheen to the fur.

COLOR: Bright Blue.

*Scottish Fold*

- Unique appearance
- Sweet temperament; likes people

- Healthy and sturdy
- Friendly with children and other pets
- Moderately quiet
- Shorthaired; easy to groom, although ears need frequent attention

All Scottish Folds can trace their pedigree back to "Susie," a folded-eared kitten that occurred as a spontaneous mutation in a litter of normal-eared farm cats in 1961. The breed was established by crosses to various shorthairs.

Scottish Folds are shorthaired cats with small, round-tipped ears that fold downward and forward, and look like a close-fitting cap on top of the head. Everything about the breed gives the impression of roundness: round, well-padded body; round paws; well-rounded head with firm chin and jaw; and expressive, round eyes that are separated by a short, broad nose. The short hair is dense and resilient.

COLORS: White, Black, Blue, Red, Cream, Chinchilla, Shaded Silver, Shell Cameo (Red Chinchilla), Shaded Cameo (Red Shaded), Black Smoke, Blue Smoke, Cameo Smoke (Red Smoke), Classic Tabby Pattern, Mackerel Tabby Pattern, Patched Tabby Pattern, Spotted Tabby Pattern, Silver Tabby, Red Tabby, Brown Tabby, Blue Tabby, Cream Tabby, Cameo Tabby, Tortoiseshell, Calico, Dilute Calico, Blue-Cream, Bi-Color, and OSFC (Other Scottish Fold Colors)—any other color or pattern with the exception of those showing evidence of hybridization resulting in the colors chocolate, lavender, the Himalayan pattern, or these combinations with white.

### *Siamese*

- Extremely intelligent; very trainable
- People-oriented; dislikes isolation
- Very affectionate; extremely demanding
- Energetic; clever; acrobatic talents
- Loud and expressive; most talkative of cat breeds
- Shorthaired; easy to groom

Although Siamese are of Eastern origin, their early history is obscure. It is known that they were highly prized in Siam hundreds of years ago because they are mentioned and depicted in old manuscripts. The first recorded American Siamese belonged to Mrs. Rutherford B. Hayes, wife of the nineteenth President of the United States.

Siamese are svelte and refined cats with long, tubular bodies; long and slim legs (their hind legs are slightly higher than the forelegs); dainty, oval paws; and long, thin, whiplike tails. They have long, tapering, wedge-shaped heads. The wedge starts at the nose and flares out in straight lines to the tips of the ears, forming a triangle. Their ears are strikingly large and pointed, and their deep-blue, almond-shaped eyes slant toward the nose. The fur is fine and glossy. The lighter body color is accentuated by darker points or extremities: facial mask, ears, legs, feet, and tail.

COLORS: Seal Point, Chocolate Point, Blue Point, and Lilac Point.

## Singapura

- Intelligent; trainable
- Loving and devoted
- Loves human companionship
- Friendly with children and other pets
- Quiet, melodious voice
- Very short, fine coat; easy to groom

The Singapura, a natural breed from the island of Singapore, was first seen in the United States in 1975. Its name is the Malaysian word for Singapore. In its native country, many Singapuras roam free; they are known as "Drain Cats" because they take refuge in drains. The CFA has recently granted the Singapura provisional status.

The Singapura is a small-sized cat with a moderately stocky and muscular body, and heavy legs that taper to small, short oval feet. The slender tail should reach the shoulder when laid across the torso. The skull is rounded, with the width at the outer eye narrowing to a definite whisker break and a medium-short, broad muzzle with a blunt nose. The noticeably large, almond-shaped eyes can be hazel, green, or yellow. The ears are large and slightly pointed. The fine, very short coat is ticked like that of an Abyssinian.

COLOR: Dark brown ticking on a warm, old ivory ground color.

## *Somali*

- Very intelligent; trainable
- Affectionate; gentle; sweet-natured
- Healthy
- Friendly with children
- Moderately quiet
- Medium-long hair; needs regular grooming

The Somali is a longhaired version of the Abyssinian cat. The breed was developed from longhaired kittens that appeared in Abyssinian litters and was recognized for championship competition by the CFA in 1978. Its name is not related to its area of origin, since most Somalis can trace their ancestry back to British cats.

Somalis are well-proportioned, medium to large, lithe but muscular cats. The body is long and graceful with a rounded rib cage. The back is slightly arched, creating the appearance of a cat about to spring. Its legs and bushy tail are in proportion to its torso. The head is a modified, slightly rounded wedge. The almond-shaped eyes may be gold or green—the richer and deeper the better. The ears are large and moderately pointed, and furnished with long tufts. The soft, dense, medium-length coat may be slightly shorter on the shoulders, but long ear tufts, a ruff, and breeches are very desirable.

COLORS: Blue, Ruddy, and Red.

### *Tonkinese*

- Very intelligent; trainable
- Meticulous habits
- Energetic; gregarious; likes attention
- Very affectionate; friendly with children and other pets
- Very talkative
- Short, fine coat; easy to groom

The Tonkinese was created in the 1960s and 1970s in Canada and the United States by crossing Siamese and Burmese. It strikes a mid-point in almost all respects between these two breeds.

The Tonkinese has a medium-length torso, well-developed but not coarse, with fairly slim legs that are proportionate to the body in length and bone. The hind legs should be slightly longer than those in front. The head is a modified wedge—a little longer than it is wide—with high cheekbones, blunt muzzle and chin, and medium-sized ears with oval tips. The almond-shaped, blue-green eyes are slightly rounded on the bottom, giving the Tonkinese a more open appearance than that of Oriental-type cats. The coat is soft and furlike in texture.

COLORS: Natural Mink, Champagne Mink, Blue Mink, Honey Mink, and Platinum Mink.

### *Turkish Angora*

- Very intelligent; trainable
- Lively and playful
- Gentle disposition
- Affectionate and devoted; often becomes attached to one person

- Quiet; gentle voice
- Medium-long to long silky hair; not as long or thick as Persians', but requires frequent grooming

One of the oldest longhaired breeds, the Angora has been known in Europe since the sixteenth century. Its name is another form of Ankara, the Turkish capital. The breed almost disappeared because of the preference for Persians, until the Ankara Zoo began a carefully controlled breeding program in the 1950s to ensure its survival.

The Turkish Angora is a medium-sized cat with a long, graceful body; long legs (the hind legs are longer than those in front); and a long, tapering tail. The small to medium-sized head is wedge-shaped. The large, almond-shaped eyes slant slightly upward. The long, pointed ears are set high on the head and are erect. Angoras have a very fine, silky, medium-length coat with a longer ruff around the neck, tufts on the ears, and a full brush on the tail.

COLORS: White, Black, Blue, Cream, Red, Black Smoke, Blue Smoke, Classic Tabby Pattern, Mackerel Tabby Pattern, Silver Tabby, Red Tabby, Brown Tabby, Blue Tabby, Cream Tabby, Tortoiseshell, Calico, Dilute Calico, Blue-Cream, and Bi-Color.

## ADDITIONAL CAT BREEDS

Here are some brief descriptions of breeds that are recognized by organizations other than the Cat Fanciers' Association, plus a few new or rare breeds.

## Cymric

The tailless Cymric is also known as a longhaired Manx. Longhaired kittens had appeared from time to time in litters of shorthaired Manx, and in the 1960s breeders opted to establish the variety as a separate breed. Its name is a derivation of *Cymru*, the Welsh name for Wales.

Aside from its medium-long coat (which comes in a variety of colors and patterns), thick jowls, and tufted ears, the Cymric closely resembles the Manx: large, round head with round muzzle and prominent cheekbones; large, expressive eyes; short, thick neck; broad chest; short back; rounded rump; deep flanks; and rounded, muscular thighs. Like the Manx, there is a decided hollow at the end of the backbone where a tail would normally begin.

Cymrics are loving and devoted cats that make charming companions. They are quiet, and they get along well with children and other pets. Their medium-long hair requires frequent grooming.

## Norwegian Forest Cat

The Norwegian Forest Cat, or *Norsk Skaukatt*, originated in Norway several centuries ago, possibly from both farm and semiwild stock. It is an extremely healthy and hardy breed, similar in appearance to the Maine Coon, although the two breeds are not related. Its shaggy, two-layered weatherproof coat—a thick and woolly undercoat to provide warmth, and a long, glistening topcoat to repel the rain or snow—is the result of decades of life in the bitter Scandinavian climate. Despite its length, the hair of Norwegian Forest Cats does not mat readily and is reasonably easy to care for.

This is a muscular, well-built cat with a long body, long legs, and wide, heavy paws. The hind legs are longer than the forelegs, making the rump higher than the shoulders. The head is triangular-shaped with full cheeks, large eyes, long and high-set ears, and a heavy chin. Any coat color or pattern is acceptable. Norwegian Forest Cats are very intelligent and energetic. They like the outdoors and are adept tree climbers. They also make excellent mousers.

### Ragdoll

Ragdolls are cats with medium-to-long hair that resembles rabbit fur. They were developed in California during the late 1960s and named because of their ability to go limp, like a ragdoll hanging over the arm, when held. Ragdolls appear to feel no pain or fear, and will refuse to defend themselves when confronted. As a result, they are extremely vulnerable animals. Because they will not protect themselves, and their injuries may go unseen, they must be checked frequently for signs of illness or injury.

These large and docile cats are often mistaken for Birmans. Ragdolls are much larger than Birmans, however, with heavier bodies, broader heads, and thicker fur. Ragdolls come in three coat patterns: Colorpoint, Mitted (white mittens on both front paws with matching white boots on hind legs), and Bi-Color, and all of them may be colored Blue Point, Chocolate Point, Seal Point, or Lilac Point. They are intelligent and extremely placid creatures that are very devoted. In the words of their breeder, "they are the closest one can get to a real live baby and still have an animal."

### *Snowshoe*

The Snowshoe is a recently developed hybrid that was produced by crossing Siamese with bi-colored American Shorthairs. A white muzzle and white feet give this charming breed a unique look.

The Snowshoe is a modified Oriental-type cat with a well-muscled and powerful body, long and solid legs with well-rounded paws, and a medium-long, slightly tapering tail. The head is a triangular-shaped wedge with a medium-long nose. The deep, vivid blue eyes are almond-shaped and slant upward from the nose to the ear. The large ears are broad at the base and pointed. The coat is short and glossy. Snowshoes come in two colors: Seal Point—a warm fawn body shading to a paler fawn on the chest and stomach with points (except for the feet and muzzle) of deep seal brown—and Blue Point—a bluish white body shading to a lighter color on the chest and stomach, with points (except for the feet and muzzle) of dark, grayish blue.

Snowshoes are energetic creatures that make charming and affectionate pets. They love to talk to their owners, although they're not as loud or as long-winded as Siamese.

### *Sphinx*

The hairless Sphinx (sometimes spelled Sphynx) is also called the Canadian Hairless and the Moon Cat. Although it resembles the descriptions of an extinct hairless cat that belonged to the Aztecs, the breed developed from a mutant hairless kitten born in a litter of shorthaired cats in Canada in 1966.

The quiet and sweet-natured Sphinx is a muscular, medium-boned, barrel-chested cat—higher in the rear—

with a long and tapering tail. The head is a rounded wedge shape, with a short nose and very large, broad-based ears with rounded tips. Of all the cat breeds, the Sphinx has to be the most bizarre-looking. It is completely hairless except for a fine, plush down on the face (this down is longest and heaviest on the nose and sides of the mouth), the back of the ears, the paws and legs up to the wrist and ankles, the tail tip, and the testicles of males. The fine down looks like velvet and feels like moss. There are no whiskers or eyebrows. The skin is taut in adults with wrinkles on the head.

Sphinx cats come in a variety of colors and patterns. No combing or brushing is required. Because of their higher body temperature, Sphinx cats sweat, and dander or any secretions that accumulate on the skin should be sponged off with warm water. A gentle massage with a little baby oil will help keep the skin from becoming rough and dry.

# A Selected Bibliography

The following interesting and recent books on cats and cat care are recommended for further reading.

Berwick, Ray and Karen Thure. *Ray Berwick's Complete Guide to Training Your Cat*. Tucson: HP Books, 1986.

Caras, Roger. *A Celebration of Cats*. New York: Simon and Schuster, 1986.

Frazier, Anitra with Norma Eckroate. *The Natural Cat—A Holistic Guide for Finicky Owners* (Revised Edition). New York: Kampmann & Co., 1983.

Kay, William J. and Elizabeth Randolph. *The Complete Book of Cat Health*. New York: Macmillan, 1985.

Kritsick, Stephen M. *Dr. Kritsick's Tender Loving Cat Care*. New York: Linden Press/Simon and Schuster, 1986.

Leyhausen, Paul. *Cat Behavior: The Predatory and Social Behavior of Domestic and Wild Cats*. New York: Garland STPM Press, 1979.

Loeb, Jo and Paul. *You Can Train Your Cat*. New York: Simon and Schuster, 1977.

Morris, Desmond. *Catwatching*. London: Jonathan Cape, 1986.

Pirotin, Debra and Sherry Suib Cohen. *No Naughty Cats*. New York: Harper & Row, 1985.

Pugnetti, Gino. *Simon and Schuster's Guide to Cats*. New York: Simon and Schuster, 1983.

Siegal, Mordecai. *The Good Cat Book*. New York: Simon and Schuster, 1981.

Suares, Jean-Claude. *The Indispensable Cat*. New York: Stewart, Tabori and Chang, 1983.

Wilbourn, Carole C. *Cats on the Couch*. New York: Macmillan, 1982.

Wright, Michael and Sally Walter, Editors. *The Book of the Cat*. New York: Summit Books, 1980.

# Index

# Index

# DON'T MISS
## THESE CURRENT
## Bantam Bestsellers